# Lewis.Tsurumaki.Lewis

# Lewis.Tsurumaki.Lewis

## Intensities

Paul Lewis, Marc Tsurumaki, David J. Lewis

Princeton Architectural Press
New York

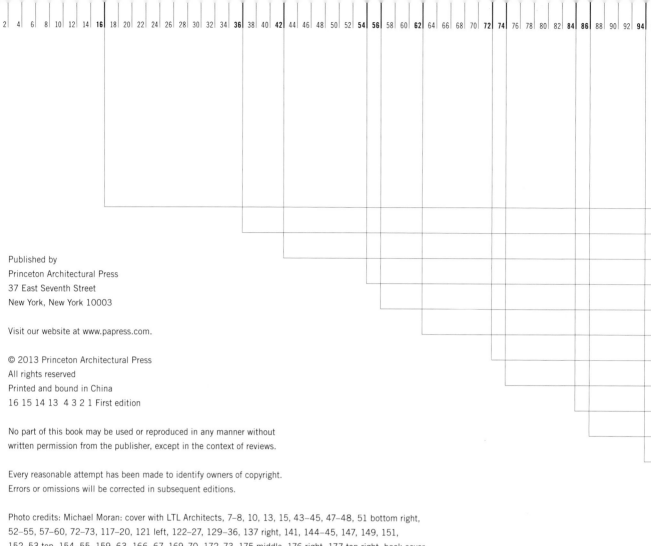

Published by
Princeton Architectural Press
37 East Seventh Street
New York, New York 10003

Visit our website at www.papress.com.

Photo credits: Michael Moran: cover with LTL Architects, 7–8, 10, 13, 15, 43–45, 47–48, 51 bottom right,
52–55, 57–60, 72–73, 117–20, 121 left, 122–27, 129–36, 137 right, 141, 144–45, 147, 149, 151,
152–53 top, 154–55, 159–63, 166–67, 169–70, 172–73, 175 middle, 176 right, 177 top right, back cover;
Elliott Kaufman: 11; dBox: 15; Florian Idenburg: 62 bottom; David Sundberg/Esto: 84–85; Alex Terzich: 87;
Barry Halkin: 88 top, 88 bottom left, 89 top, 89 bottom right, back cover; Richard Barnes: 112–13;
Luke Gibson: 114 bottom right; Diana Mera Hernando: 184–85

LTL would like to thank Elizabeth Kuwada, Kristen Chin, Carrie Schulz, Jason Dannenbring, John Morrison,
Kevin Hayes, Keith Greenwald, Diana Mera Hernando, and Constanza Cortes for their work on this book.

Editor: Megan Carey
Editorial Assistant: Gina Morrow
Design: Lewis.Tsurumaki.Lewis

Special thanks to: Bree Anne Apperley, Sara Bader, Nicola Bednarek Brower, Janet Behning, Fannie Bushin,
Carina Cha, Andrea Chlad, Benjamin English, Russell Fernandez, Will Foster, Jan Haux, Diane Levinson,
Jennifer Lippert, Jacob Moore, Katharine Myers, Margaret Rogalski, Elana Schlenker, Dan Simon,
Sara Stemen, Andrew Stepanian, Paul Wagner, and Joseph Weston of Princeton Architectural Press
—Kevin C. Lippert, publisher

Library of Congress Cataloging-in-Publication Data
Lewis, Paul, 1966–
 Lewis.Tsurumaki.Lewis : intensities / Paul Lewis, Marc Tsurumaki, David J. Lewis. — 1st edition.
    pages  cm
  ISBN 978-1-61689-066-7 (pbk.)
  1. Lewis.Tsurumaki.Lewis. 2. Architecture, Modern—21st century. I. Tsurumaki, Marc, 1965–
II. Lewis, David J., 1966– III. Title.
  NA737.L454L465 2012
  720.92'2—dc23
                                                      2012019308

# Contents

# Introduction

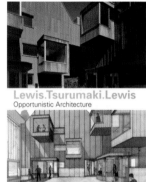

*Situation Normal...* (1998)                    *Opportunistic Architecture* (2008)

In adopting the word *intensities* as the title of this monograph, we seek the full and varied meaning of the term: at once that which is intense and the context that makes intensity legible. To intensify something is to call attention to it by altering the thing itself or else the frame in which it is understood. *Intensities* aptly describes how LTL Architects practices architecture and defines our goals for transformation through architecture. The plural form of the word reflects the multiple levels of intensity within our work. This design process is a focused form of architectural practice; with relentless curiosity, we engage the pragmatics of a given project, pursuing design invention through a nonlinear yet logical sequence of speculations and probes. The work that materializes is then saturated, multilayered, or otherwise demonstrative of an intensification of architecture itself. This is not to conflate intensity with pure excess or plenitude. Rather, we are interested in the set of relations intensity implies: selective minimization can be equally effective in creating structures of intensity. Intensity can mean less and not just more.

The term we've adopted captures interlinked aspects of our architectural practice, outlined here in five categories: 1) Intensities of Contingency points to our commitment to researching the constraints of any given project and to a design method that arises from a project's contingencies; 2) Intensities of Resources highlights our belief that material limitations and economic constraints drive architecture in a time of heightened environmental awareness; 3) Intensities of Section foregrounds the crucial role that section plays in our work as the precise site for experimentation with space, form, performance, and representation; 4) Intensities of Surface captures our interest in the material invention and development of skins, walls, and boundaries that define architecture and in turn determine the intensity of perception and use; and 5) Intensities of the Social focuses on the consequences of design, underscoring our belief in architecture's capacity to transform daily life.

*Intensities* builds on the material we documented in two previous publications. *Pamphlet Architecture 21: Situation Normal...* (1998) presented projects in which New York City served as a testing ground for new organizations that exploited the peculiarities overlooked in urban habits. Working primarily through techniques of architectural representation, we wanted to develop a "surrational" architecture: It would take seriously the underpinnings of programs in order to push architectural propositions catalyzed by the density of Manhattan to the point of the absurd. Ten years later, *Opportunistic Architecture* (2008) integrated text, hybrid drawing techniques, and photography of built work to argue for placing the architect as an

**Bornhuetter Hall**

**Building 82%**

**Dash Dogs**

opportunistic agent within a field of given conditions. We approached architecture as a multivalent discipline that is most fascinating when it embraces a plurality of concerns, even if they are contradictory. In this book, we continue to explore a complex, critical, playful, and opportunistic approach to our practice. Framing the role of the architect within the political, economic, social, and cultural constraints of a specific project, our work transforms these conditions. Instead of constructing the firm's identity through reductive clarity, we make legible those architectural effects that are fundamentally messy and nuanced.

Since we founded the firm in 1997, we have pursued an intentionally broad array of projects in the belief that architecture has the capacity to impact daily life at various scales through distinct programs. Our projects have ranged from furniture to infrastructural landscapes, from speculative self-generated projects to tectonically explicit buildings for institutions. While the projects in this book are typically of greater scale and complexity, LTL's commitment to engaging public and accessible work is consistent. A significant percentage is in fact the result of collaborations between LTL and academic institutions that appreciate the role of architecture in establishing the spatial and cultural field of educational discourse. All three principals hold long-standing positions in higher education and understand architecture to be a practice and a form of pedagogy. Faced with the range of choices, questions, and obligations of contemporary architectural practice, we believe it is not sufficient simply to do work. Architectural projects have their greatest impact when a clear argument or line of inquiry drives the decision-making process and then registers in the structures of intensification that establish hierarchy, meaning, and importance.

### Intensities of Contingency

Meaningful research requires curiosity and inclusiveness, encouraged by a suspension of previous assumptions. We begin each project through research into its unique parameters. By "research," we mean both the gathering and collecting of information, data, and facts and the use of initial architectural designs to probe and push assumptions. At the outset, we seek a density of information to frame the conditions of the project, raising the issues of budget, schedule, expected uses, codes, environmental impacts, and aesthetic demands to inform even early architectural propositions, rather than adhering to a singular focus, medium, or approach. These multiple contingencies invariably circumscribe the development of design; they must be negotiated, but they can also be generatively exploited. Intensity is therefore both a precondition of the architectural project and a selective operation,

**Fluff Bakery**

**FAAR-Out**

the leveraging of various conditions and parameters to allow the most productive trajectories to emerge. Even when some parameters recede based on the research and testing of design possibilities, no contingency can be dismissed, compromised, or flattened out. In this way, environmental conditions may become the primary motive, as in Water Proving Ground, our project for New Jersey's Liberty State Park, while the need to reinforce a client's mission may also become dominant, as in the Open Planning Project.

We maintain that architectural design is a critical form of research that establishes a feedback loop that brings clients' and users' insights and responses into the design process. Architectural proposals are factually informed speculations that in turn qualify the assumptions regarding the project held by client, architect, and design team. This research knits together analysis and projection, with the architect serving as pragmatic alchemist. Intensities therefore imply a judicious approach that acknowledges complexities while operating selectively, tuning various factors up or down to allow for the emergence of the most compelling proposal. This means resisting any singular, reductive strategy or facile answer, such that a given project simply carries out a rehearsed plan. Instead, we always favor the cultivation of paradox and contradiction over singular goals.

This type of research—framed by design as research and research informing design—is underwritten by our insistence on a nonlinear but thoroughly logical pursuit of architectural invention. We work through an iterative design process akin to testing, forming a collaborative design team around each project. Each team explores multiple incremental shifts and modifications and externalizes them for open interpretation and reinvention. One iterative test creates opportunities for subsequent exploration and testing, so the design develops through invention sprawl; one challenge is met with multiple options that in turn lead to further inquiry and subsequent speculation. Like Theseus's pursuit of the Minotaur, the operation can be retraced from the end point, but the path and its ends are never known or envisioned from the start. Our amplification of logic upends the commonly held belief that the best design averages demands and synthesizes competing problems through a single sketch or proposal. We instead seek to harness the often conflicting demands of a project, holding these demands in creative tension until the final realization. The manner in which we see design invention driven by a conscious set of decisions derives from the structure of the LTL office. Invention does not flow from the fountainhead of a single author. Rather, the three principals collaborate, in concert with the assembled project team drawn from members of

**Geltner Loft**

Great Egyptian Museum

the office and outside consultants, to set the direction of every project. These teams have grown in scale and complexity, a reflection of the increased level of work in the office and of the rising regulatory and technical demands of architectural practice today. The growth of specialized knowledge means that the project that in 2002 required only a small team now may require three times the people. Rather than lamenting the architect's loss of authority, we argue that only a methodology that embraces this very complexity will be effective in ascribing agency to the architect in the design process. Our work thus emerges out of discourse, not dictation. Design team members representing various areas of knowledge and expertise constitute a forum in which they can argue for different levels of intensification with respect to the given contingencies; the architect orchestrates the debated contingencies into the final project. Recently, ecological and economic constraints have become more important for all members of the design team.

### Intensities of Resources

Countering the proposition that architectural significance correlates to dollars per square foot, we believe that financial boundaries sharpen the design process; they aid the quality of the architecture rather than limit it. The majority of the work in this book was executed during the economic recession that followed the financial crisis of fall 2008. All of the projects were subject to the fiscal contingency of constrained budgets. The judicious use of resources is therefore foregrounded in this work, which accentuates select aspects for maximum effect. We put the money where it will have the greatest impact on the utility, perception, and life of any given project, and we downplay other areas within the same project to heighten that effect. From the design of large spaces that can accommodate a vast range of uses to the detailing of individual components that perform in numerous ways, we seek excess through economy. For example, rather than making the existing Arthouse at the Jones Center building appear new at high cost, we tactically inserted selective details and components into the existing shell. These insertions focused the use of resources while transforming the entire building. Ultimately they furthered the trajectory of the building's history rather than calcifying a moment in time. Constrained budgets encourage inventive, hybrid solutions; they have reinforced a consistent aspect of our work, which is to do more with "less is more" through a multiplication of function.

Resource limitations dictate that the desired material richness come via design invention. We continue to explore the creation of complex surfaces from materials usually considered ordinary, often through repetition and accumulation; through intensification, these surfaces

Ini Ani Coffee Shop

Lozoo Restaurant

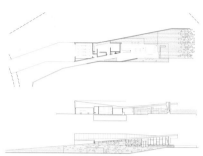

Nazareth House

achieve effects not initially associated with a given material. One such transformation is visible in the shifting cedar wall and felt-lined recycled-bottle acoustic baffles for the Claremont University Consortium (CUC) Administrative Campus Center; another appears in the cork-clad wall and floor for New York University's Department of Social and Cultural Analysis (SCA). We also work in the opposite direction, intentionally downplaying specific surfaces in order to highlight areas or objects of focus. We embrace the challenge of material and energy intensification as a critical strategy for addressing holistically the question of future sustainability, predicated on maximizing impact through a minimum of means. We evaluate each project on its own terms to avoid inflexible standards or ideological positions. This propels us into architecture that is vibrant and engaged, an architecture that strives to exceed any basic system of check-off points. The insistence on a multiplicity of performance not only reduces material outlay, but also fosters a layering of use that changes with the cycles of daily life. In the case of the CUC project, we achieved the greatest impact by maximizing the daylight within a deep floor plate to radically cut energy use. In the case of the Gallaudet University Living and Learning Residence Hall 6 (LLRH6), we used robust construction systems to ensure the long life of the building.

Exploiting the potential of repurposing buildings will be an increasingly dominant architectural challenge as the true life-cycle costs of buildings force a reevaluation of the culture of newness that has driven disposable building practices. Architects must be nimble and inventive when creating a contemporary building from structures and shells that are antithetical to the desired use. Many of our projects, including Arthouse, the CUC, the Sullivan Family Student Center for the University of Wyoming, and New York University's SCA and Office of Strategic Assessment, Planning and Design (SAPD), have been framed by this condition. In each case, we had to find the maximal utility of the existing space while holding in creative tension the legacy of the past with the obligations of future occupation. In each case, the apparent incompatibility of the requested program and the given site conditions led not only to a great efficiency of resources, but also to an illogical yet wonderful friction between the existing structure and its new uses. It is precisely that friction that we exploit for new spatial and performative effects, often played out through section.

## Intensities of Section

Section is the representational means to make visible the most complex and intriguing aspects of architecture. In our work, it is both an instrumental tool and the site

New Suburbanism

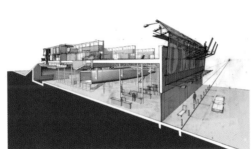

Parking Sections

of much of our design effort. Whereas plan typically provides the means to choreograph program, section is where thermal forces, building form, and structural and material systems converge and are most legible. As computer modeling has increasingly served as the dominant design tool over the past twenty years, diagrams and renderings have proliferated within the discourse. Whereas the diagram is abstract, the rendering is specific. Yet both are inadequate for engaging the complexities of tectonics, the resistance of materials, and the definition of interior space. Section, and specifically section perspective, engages these challenges much better. Moreover, in an urban context, it reveals and explores the spatial and human density enabled through multiple-level construction and design.

If the plan examines questions of circulation and movement, the section explores the body's proportional and functional relationship to the spatial and material conditions of architecture. Section makes tangible the basic conditions of the natural environment, from the sun's changing altitude to gravity's pull on moisture and structure. To foster our exploration of architecture through section, we have categorized the section into seven dominant types: extrude, stack, shape, shear, hole, incline, and nest. These types allow us to take advantage of new combinations and models, thus intensifying the section's agency in our work.

The extrusion of a plan to a height sufficient for the intended activity is the most basic form of a section. An extruded section has little to no variation in the vertical axis, and the vast majority of buildings are based on a maximally efficient ratio of square footage to building volume. Although it is a section type, an extruded section lacks spatial complexity. Stacking is an extruded section that is capable of being deployed ad nauseum. It fulfills a basic purpose of section, which is to increase the real estate value of the land through repetition of floor plates; a stacked section by itself rarely contains interior vertical effects. Shaping is a modulation of the horizontal surface. It adds a particular volume to the section and can occur in the floor, the ceiling, or both. Buildings with shaped sections often exhibit a close fit of structure and section. Shear induces a rift or cut parallel to the horizontal or vertical axis of section. It is particularly effective at inducing optical, thermal, or acoustic connections within an extruded or stacked section without significantly compromising the tectonic efficiencies of the repetitions upon which those types are based. Holes penetrate slabs and are frequently used to exchange floor area for benefits in section. They range in scale and quantity from single, small openings between floors to multiple, large atria that organize whole buildings. Inclines change the angle of the plan and are a means of continuing a

**Park Tower**

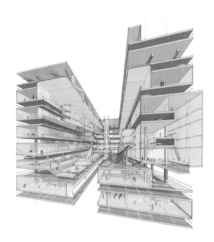

Refiled

horizontal section surface; in so doing, they push the plan into a section that can be occupied. With inclines, section does not require the sacrifice of any portion of the plan. Finally, nests produce section through the interplay or overlap of discrete volumes. The structural and environmental performance of the nest usually exceeds that of the volumes in isolation.

Each of these seven types can be broken into a range of variations; more importantly the types combine in multiple ways. Indeed, buildings that manifest intriguing sections rarely contain just one type of section. For example, Frank Lloyd Wright's Guggenheim Museum combines an incline and a hole that facilitates physical continuity in the ramp and optical continuity across the atrium. We used this section hybrid as a point of departure for the New Taipei City Museum of Art; our variation makes a void of the incline section, embedding it within a stacked and sheared section to produce moments of discontinuity within and adjacencies between disparate programs. Rather than locate the incline immediately above another incline (which, in effect, produces a stacked, albeit sloped, section), we articulated the ceiling above the incline as a shaped section to induce specific, focused rooms within the unfolding sequence. This intensification of section is evident in almost all of our work. Arthouse, for example, is an existing stacked section that we animated through

holes: the central stair, a shaped section at the entry, and a nested section in the community-room volume. The Grid and the Superblock combines two types and scales of incline, perpendicular to one another, that intersect a stacked section and are activated with myriad holes. For Water Proving Ground, we were concerned less with a multiplicity of section types and effects than with the development of a single type. Through an exhaustive exploration of inclined planes and surfaces, we determined that even a one-foot change in sea level would have dramatic consequences for the sloping, amphibious landscape that formed the basis of our design.

In projects constrained to a single floor, the ceiling has become for us the site of design experimentation in a direct challenge to the proliferation of the dropped ceiling in contemporary building culture. Although the ceiling has a long history as the site of spatial experimentation, cultural value, and structural complexity—take, for example, Gothic cathedrals—the ceiling's potential is rarely leveraged for effects now. The ubiquitous dropped ceiling is the perfect barometer of this banality and therefore ripe for reexamination. At its most basic, the dropped ceiling conceals the expanding mechanical infrastructure required in contemporary buildings; at the same time, it privileges the dominance of plan over the interior spatial definition created through section. Its grid ruthlessly marks the eradication

**Tides Restaurant**

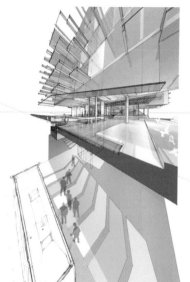

**Tourbus Hotel**

of section, the denial of tectonics, and the material opportunities of the interior. In almost every one of our interior projects, we have exploited a reflected ceiling plan to induce section effects within the space. Unlike the floor plans, which are predetermined by circulation patterns and code requirements, the ceiling is often available for sculptural transformation, reinforcing and extending the acoustic, lighting, spatial, and material qualities of a given project. In many of our projects, notably the Buffet at MGM CityCenter and the CUC, the complexity of the ceiling exceeds the manipulation of plan and the ground floor, where ceiling transformations define spatial volumes that float above more open floor layouts. The ceiling, however, is only one of the intensified surfaces that welcomes invention.

## Intensities of Surface

Over the last four decades, architectural discourse about surface has polarized: Surface has come to be understood either as semiotically encoded cladding or as a tectonic and performative composition. The projects in this book challenge the now-established binary by engaging both positions in any given design, conflating operational and representational functions within a single complex membrane. The multivalent surfaces that result provide a legible armature for spatial and programmatic organizations while integrating diverse,

contradictory functional requirements and heightened material and perceptual effects.

While the continuous surface has become a formal cliché in the early twenty-first century, we remain interested in advancing the possibilities of the contiguous surface. Fascinated less by its formal capacity than its programmatic ambiguities, we push continuity toward dense performance. We seek complex surfaces that at their best serve spatial roles of enclosure, division, and delineation yet incorporate a variety of technical and programmatic needs, including acoustic control, thermal performance, lighting and light manipulation, ergonomic support, and visual separation. The hybrid conditions that result are neither pure figuration nor the outcome of simple operational determinants; their intentional ambiguity straddles the line between figure and performance. For instance, the single, dominant wall of SAPD at NYU simultaneously operates as an identifiable marker that organizes the office space and as an acoustic and pinnable surface that displays the work of the office it organizes.

One of the most significant aspects of these surfaces' performance is their direct engagement of the user. The functional amplification of these architectural elements enables the individual subject to encounter the surface physically in both conventional and unexpected ways. Seating, steps, counters, and other

**Tourbus Hotel**

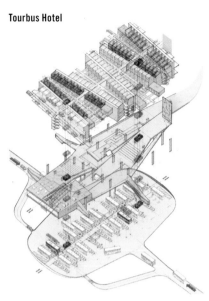

**Upside House**

**Van Alen Institute**

functional elements typically conceived of as independent or supplemental are assimilated into the composite surface, thus blurring the line between architecture and furniture. In these cases, we modify the condition of the wall through splitting or thickening, so that as surface and as space, the wall can accommodate the user. At NYU's SCA, for example, one may sit against, pass through, or occupy the interior of the main feature wall, intensifying the relationship between the occupant and the material condition of the architecture.

These dense surfaces are also articulated relative to their material and tectonic assembly. They activate both haptic and optical levels of engagement as the material invention challenges the user's perception of space throughout the changes of a day. This strategy plays upon the suggestion of surface through points, lines, or planes such that seemingly solid or homogenous features are revealed, upon closer examination, to be composed of discontinuous parts. These surfaces therefore exist at distinct scales of legibility: Whereas the overall figure and its effects are primary from a distance, a closer scale makes legible the specifics of aggregation, assembly, and attachment, as well as the material qualities of the component parts. Again, these intensifications do manifest through form, yet our interest in surface continuity extends to the tangible material and unexpected social accumulations possible therein.

## Intensities of the Social

In a world increasingly defined by virtual social networks and isolating personal technologies (smartphones, iPads, etc.), we maintain architecture's unique capacity to intensify the social through the direct organization of space. Although remote connectivity and the buffer of handheld devices are now ubiquitous, they have not supplanted extant spatial practices but rather exist alongside them. These new formats are now inscribed in the material forms of cities, buildings, and dwellings. While these technologies seem to erode the dominance of social relations based on proximity and physical gathering, their pervasiveness has paradoxically placed increasing importance on the interpersonal and the corporeal. Responding to this paradox in ways formal and contingent, at scales large and small, our projects amplify social relationships by orchestrating embodied space. Our architecture explores overlaps, combinations, and multiple uses, making one design do as much as possible through careful attention to changes in daily cycles and experience. We privilege spaces that are a good fit to multiple distinct and simultaneous programs, relying on a limited number of changeable elements— walls, screens, lights—to create dramatic change.

Our approach relies upon program as a generative condition of architectural form while it challenges any simplistic relationship between form and function.

**Vegas 888**

**Wooster House**

**Xing Restaurant**

Program in this context is more precise and expansive than its basic square-footage designations. It is more precise in the sense that direct physical engagement determines the intensified relationship with the occupant, and it is more expansive in that such a program encourages multivalence, misuse, and appropriation. In many cases, this generative condition involves an intentional doubling or multiplication of program, the finding of overlaps among uses, and the tailoring of the architecture to an intensity of habitation rather than a singularity of function. The layering of functions proliferates the possible occupations, amplifying the social potential of spaces by facilitating chance encounters in addition to structured activities. The entry lobby of Arthouse functions not only as a formal reception zone, but also as an extension of the public sidewalk beyond its transparent walls. While the space can accommodate exhibits and installations, its visual continuity with the street, its adaptable felt furniture, and its generously proportioned stair encourage a variety of inhabitations, including its use as an impromptu dance floor at the project opening. A series of public rooms in the SCA offices at NYU convert circulation into social space by opening diversely scaled spaces for collaboration and exchange within an efficiently configured plan. At the Gallaudet University LLRH6, the entry lounge is designed to extend the central campus lawn, establishing a spatial hinge between the academic life of the university and the social space of the students who reside on the floors above.

Underwriting our desire to amplify social relations is a fundamental belief in the transformative capacity of architecture within larger cultural, public, urban, and institutional frameworks. Whereas we recognize that there is no precisely quantifiable causal relationship between a space and its social effects, we also know that the relationship is not arbitrary. The value of the architecture derives from the creative transformation of the project's contingencies into the organized yet unexpected social exchanges it facilitates. It is in the execution of such transformations that we are optimistic about the architect's role as an alchemist of intensities, one who uses the full range of available resources, techniques, and systems to generate meaningful work under the ripe spatial and material conditions of architecture.

# Water Proving Ground

Liberty State Park, New Jersey

The projected inundation of the urban edge by rising sea levels has catalyzed a rethinking of the productive interplay between land and water. LTL addressed this issue as one of five firms selected by the Museum of Modern Art to participate in the workshop and exhibition *Rising Currents: Projects for New York's Waterfront*. The show examined the anticipated impact of global warming and the rising sea level on New York Harbor through a series of speculative design proposals for five sites on the water's edge. LTL was charged with the zone located in the northwest quadrant of the harbor, including Liberty State Park and New York City's iconic Liberty and Ellis Islands.

Created between 1880 and 1920 by extensive landfill operations associated with the arrival of the railroad, the site did not exist as land until the end of the nineteenth century. According to even the most conservative predictions of rising sea levels, it is currently destined to all but disappear underwater in the next fifty to seventy-five years. In response to these dire predictions, our proposal maintains the zone's public use by allowing for selective infiltration of the site by the harbor. By tactically adjusting the historic fill through subtle topographic shifts, Water Proving Ground envisions a vibrant new amphibious landscape continually activated by rising tides. Traditional defensive approaches, such as high sea walls, attempt to minimize the water's edge. However, LTL's design multiplies the length of the coastline by a factor of ten, to forty-four miles, sculpting

the site into a series of four raised landscape piers, each crenellated to generate a sawtooth interlocking of land and water. While it renders the site a more resilient buffer to storm surge and flood events, the project also maximizes the intertidal zone's capacity to serve as a testing ground for new uses and inhabitations based on the dynamic exchange between sea and land. Employing a wide range of boundary types, from hard-edge separations that isolate remediation zones to gradually sloping fields of estuarial interchange, the design actively engages tidal fluctuations, integrating water as a performative element rather than a picturesque feature.

Structured as a series of petri dishes, the plan incorporates a diversity of programs and multiple ecologies—from experimental agriculture to aquatic recreation, from tidal flats to constructed wetlands—to combine productive landscape and urban park. Further drawing public activity into the site, each of the four land piers terminates in a programmatic anchor: an aquaculture research and development center, an amphitheater and tidal park, a water lodge, and a regional produce market. Enhanced systems of aquatic- and land-based transportation link the site to both the surrounding urban context and the harbor itself, reestablishing it as a vital point of exchange within the region. In testing the opportunistic and productive exchanges created by water levels linked to global climate change, the project explores modes of coastal occupation that will become pertinent for millions of the world's citizens in the not-so-distant future.

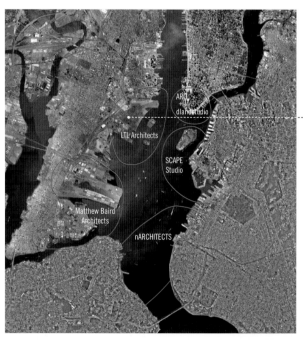

Less than 150 years ago, the site was a shallow estuarial flat, home to abundant wildlife that flourishes in zones of tidal fluctuation.

Based on conservative projections, a sea level increase of two feet is anticipated by 2080, inundating approximately 68 percent of the given site at high tide.

To facilitate ship-to-rail transfer, a successive series of landfill projects filled in the tidal basin, creating low-lying ground for more than one hundred linear miles of railroad track.

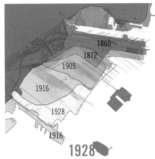

The rapid-ice-melt scenario projects a rise of four feet in sea level by 2080 and the submersion of 80 percent of the site at high tide.

The completion of the New Jersey Turnpike led to the eventual abandonment of the rail lines. In 1976, a portion of the site was turned into Liberty State Park, distinguished by an extensive crescent-shaped harbor edge.

Flooding associated with hundred-year storms will generate an eight-foot rise in sea level. By 2080, these storms will be more frequent, covering more than 95 percent of the site every fifteen years.

**Existing: five miles of coast:** The current site is defined by a hard-edged division of land and water that renders it susceptible to inundation. Because it is primarily flat, rising sea levels will have a dramatic impact on the existing park.

**Low tide: forty-five miles of coast:** Integrating a wide array of edge conditions to facilitate different levels of exchange between water and land, the new design exploits the tidal dynamics of the harbor. The coastline at low tide is ten miles longer than it is at high tide.

**Proposed: cut and fill:** From the site's existing fill alone, a new coastal profile is created, softening the edge of the site to absorb storm surge. The resulting topography is a mix of higher ground and water channels.

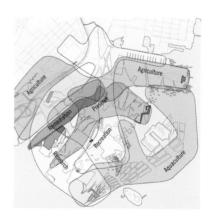

**Circulation and anchors:** Enhanced circulation routes engage the site, suturing it to neighboring urban areas and bringing together water- and land-based systems of transportation. New programmatic anchors at the end of each of the piers activate the area.

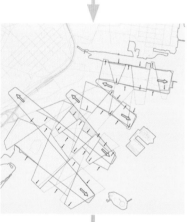

**Proposed: piers and cross grain:** The site is sculpted into four landscape piers of varying topography. To maximize the coastline, the edge of each pier is modified according to an overall sawtooth pattern.

**Program areas:** Zones of distinct use weave through the site, providing a cross section of diverse programs and activities on each pier. These uses intensify existing functions and adjacencies of the site.

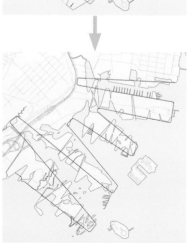

**High tide: thirty-five miles of coast:** The new plan anticipates a four-foot rise in sea level. Even at high tide, the adjusted site creates seven times the intertidal surface than in the current condition.

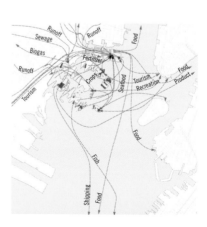

**Flows:** Tied into cycles of agriculture, aquaculture, recreation, and tourism, the redesigned site recaptures the historic role of the area as a vital point of exchange in New York Harbor.

Anticipated 2080 sea levels

Storm surge
category 2
+7'

+6'

100-year flood
+5'

Rapid ice melt
+4'

+3'

Conservative rise
+2'

+1'

High tide
+3'

+2'

+1'

Sea level
0'

-1'

-2'

-3'

Low tide
-4'

Current 2012 sea levels

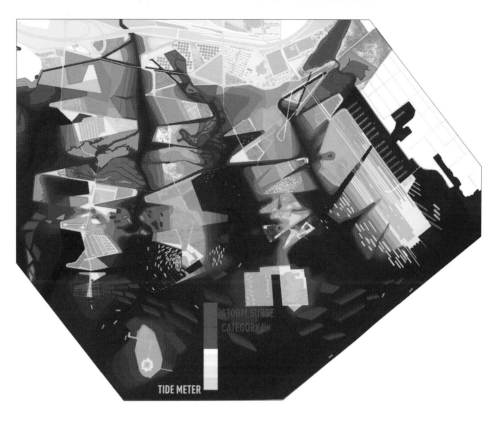

STORM SURGE
CATEGORY II

TIDE METER

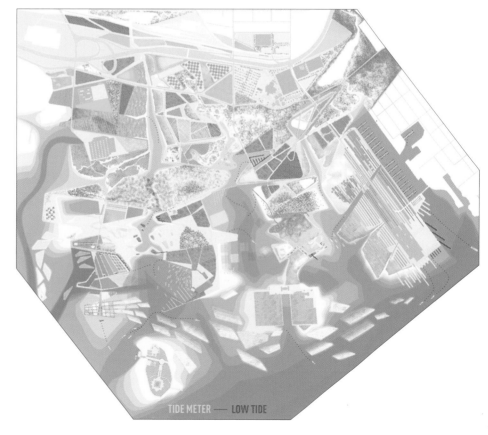

TIDE METER — LOW TIDE

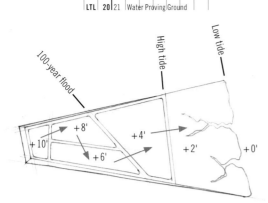

Petri dishes are isolated environments for culturing cells to facilitate tests and studies. Premised on the maximization of biodiversity, Water Proving Ground adopts the logic of the petri dish to accommodate a multiplicity of landscapes, habitats, and programs that juxtapose natural and artificial, productive and recreational, land- and water-based uses. These wedge-shaped zones comprise distinct areas, ranging in their degree of containment from the highly compartmentalized (in, for example, bioremediation areas) to the very permeable (aquaculture zones). Within each wedge, the terrain slopes from higher to lower, harnessing the dynamics of water flow and tidal change.

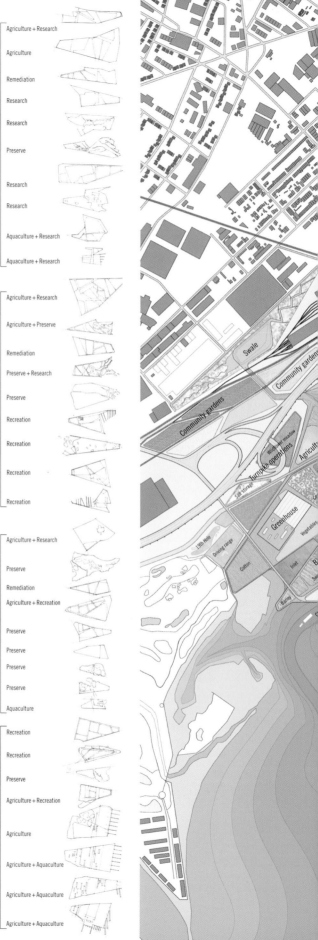

**A**
- Agriculture + Research
- Agriculture
- Remediation
- Research
- Research
- Preserve
- Research
- Research
- Aquaculture + Research
- Aquaculture + Research

**B**
- Agriculture + Research
- Agriculture + Preserve
- Remediation
- Preserve + Research
- Preserve
- Recreation
- Recreation
- Recreation
- Recreation

**C**
- Agriculture + Research
- Preserve
- Remediation
- Agriculture + Recreation
- Preserve
- Preserve
- Preserve
- Preserve
- Aquaculture

**D**
- Recreation
- Recreation
- Preserve
- Agriculture + Recreation
- Agriculture
- Agriculture + Aquaculture
- Agriculture + Aquaculture
- Agriculture + Aquaculture

The proposed aquaculture research and development center consists of a series of laboratories and testing beds located at the terminus of the southernmost pier. As the second floor and usable roof provide a stable artificial horizon, the floating docks fluctuate with the tide to allow for controlled testing of aquatic species in the estuarine environment of the harbor. Farther inland, fish hatcheries and hydrological testing facilities house various forms of marine research that utilize the harbor as an environmental and scientific resource.

An amphitheater, adjacent to Liberty Island, continues a current use of Liberty State Park by providing a venue for large-scale outdoor concerts, now redesigned to engage the harbor. Camping barges and a marina allow for concert viewing from the water, while open-air seating and sloped lawns offer land-side audiences the Statue of Liberty as a backdrop. Repositioning the floating stage generates multiple relationships between performers and audiences, and a secondary enclosed space below the amphitheater offers a more controlled venue for smaller performances.

The water lodge provides for longer-term inhabitation of the site and serves as a base for the exploration of its various landscapes. Rising out of the watery ground near Ellis Island, the building shelters a marina for kayaks, a series of flooding terraces, and recreational pools integrated into the terrain. Boardwalks, docks, and boat trails link the lodge with campsites and diverse habitats, including the Invasive Species Botanical Preserve, which maintains the unique combination of nonnative plant species that flourished on the site as a legacy of its

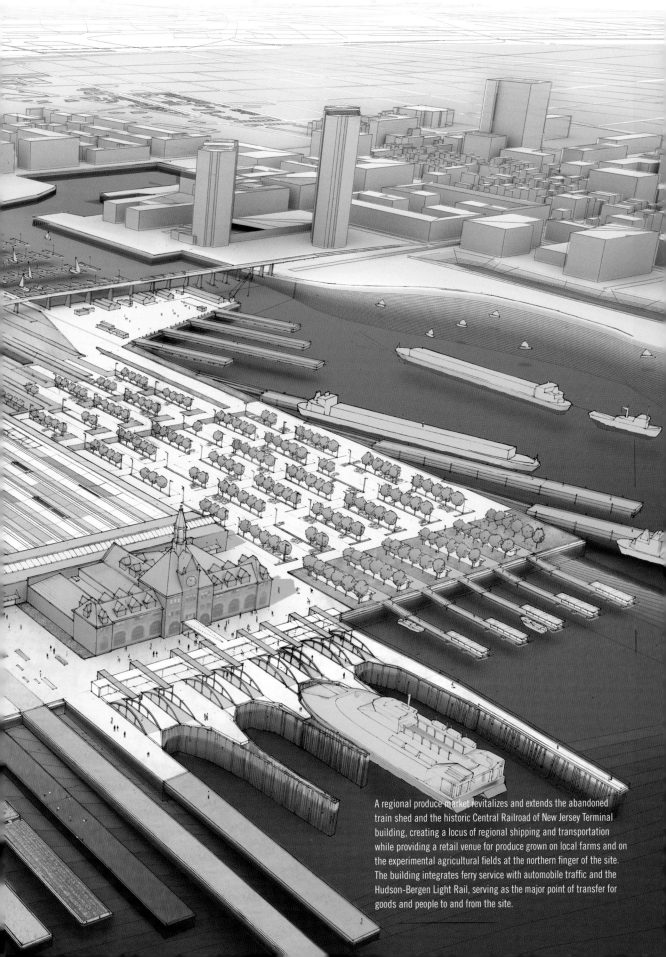

A regional produce market revitalizes and extends the abandoned train shed and the historic Central Railroad of New Jersey Terminal building, creating a locus of regional shipping and transportation while providing a retail venue for produce grown on local farms and on the experimental agricultural fields at the northern finger of the site. The building integrates ferry service with automobile traffic and the Hudson-Bergen Light Rail, serving as the major point of transfer for goods and people to and from the site.

Focused on integrated multitrophic aquaculture, the research and development center studies the interdependencies of farmed species to create a more balanced, less environmentally damaging means of cultivating the water. The network of floating walkways allows researchers, along with the general public, to access a variety of testing beds and explore multiple methods of supporting and harvesting fish and shellfish. The facility explores the possible restoration of the harbor's former role as a rich source of sustenance for the region.

A

AQUACULTURE R&D CENTER

TIDAL PARK

Up the pier from the amphitheater, a tidal park provides a shallow, watery field for recreational use, incorporating islands, pools, and beaches. The unstable terrain presents a perpetually shifting environment with landscapes that emerge and disappear with the fluctuation of the tides.

B

Extending the sloping logic of the terrain, the water lodge moves from being embedded within the landscape to being suspended above it, wrapping in plan to form an artificial cove for watercraft below. A forest of columns that support the elevated banks of rooms are also mooring posts for kayaks and other small boats and act as a launching point for excursions into the site's diverse aquatic environments. Elevated boardwalks allow for exploration on foot or bike and lead to water taxi access to other points in the harbor.

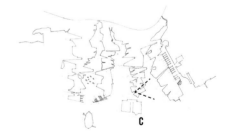

C

WATER LODGE TERRACES                    BIOREMEDIATION ZONE

On the northernmost pier, the roof system of the extant train sheds is reoccupied and extended to blend into the adjacent agrarian areas, setting the cadence for test fields of flood- and salt-resistant crops. Enclosed greenhouses and market spaces alternate with a striated landscape of variegated planting. The program interweaves agriculture, research, and commerce.

D

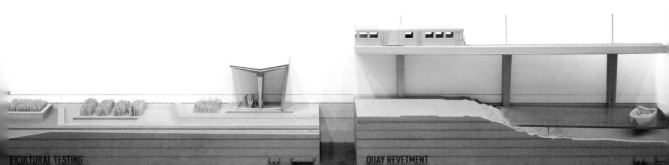

PICULTURAL TESTING        QUAY REVETMENT

Although the project depended on variations in section, the large scale
of the site required those fluctuations to be registered primarily in
plan. In other words, small changes in water level would affect large
areas of ground, which created a representational challenge. To make
the variations legible, a large-scale topographic relief model was
milled and then augmented with buildings and overlaid with line work.
To then make visible the effects of section in plan, an animation of the
transformation from low tide to high tide to storm surge was projected
onto the model.

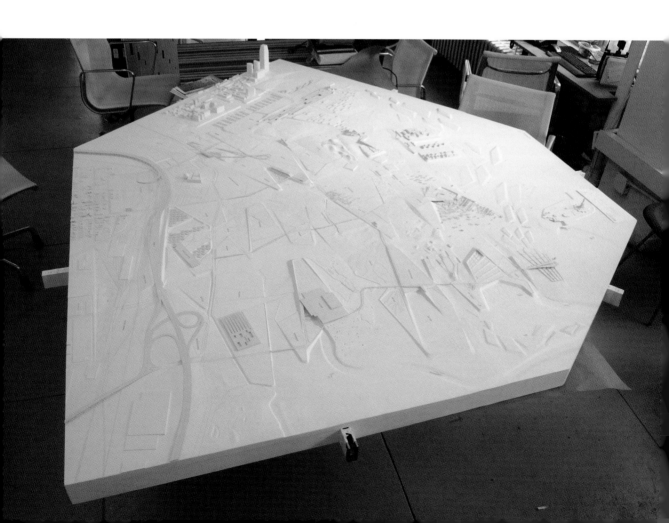

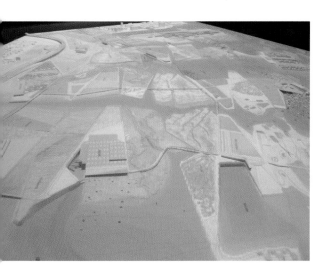

# Switchback House

Akron, Ohio

This addition to a modestly scaled single-family home in the suburbs of Akron responds to the unique pressures of its site: an otherwise typical residential lot distinguished by a precipitous ravine and a densely wooded landscape of mature trees. A guest bedroom, shop, office, and gallery nearly double the size of the existing small residence, while the form of the new structure negotiates four distinct directional pressures: a steeply rising topography to the west, automotive entry to the north, connection to the main house to the east, and engagement of the dramatic ravine views to the south. The geometry of the addition simultaneously navigates the several large specimen trees that occupy the site, minimizing tree removal and conforming to existing open areas. The resulting spatial logic derives from weaving the space of the building through the forested landscape.

      Although the client wanted the design to address the ravine, geotechnical information suggested that the bulk of the addition should pull back from the edge of the precipice. The mass of the pavilion therefore extends east to west along the long axis of the original house, and the new bedroom is located on the high ground. The addition moves out and up, expanding laterally from the public spaces of the main residence and deflecting in two directions to preserve the mature oak trees in the side yard. The Y-shaped lower level divides into a gallery and office space that opens onto the rear yard and a garage and shop facing the street. Carved into the mass of the hill, the ground-floor spaces are defined by a slate-clad retaining wall that stretches out toward the ravine.

**Site**

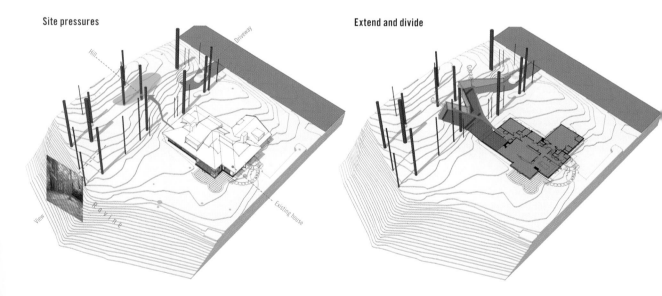

**Site pressures**

**Extend and divide**

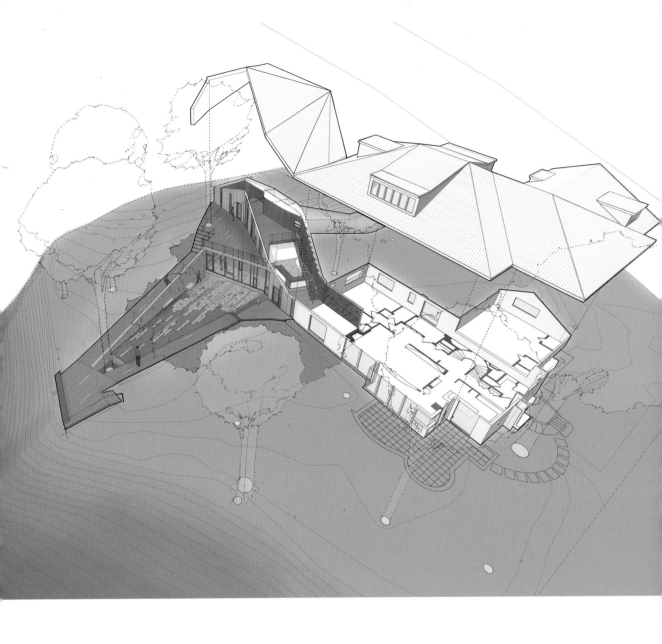

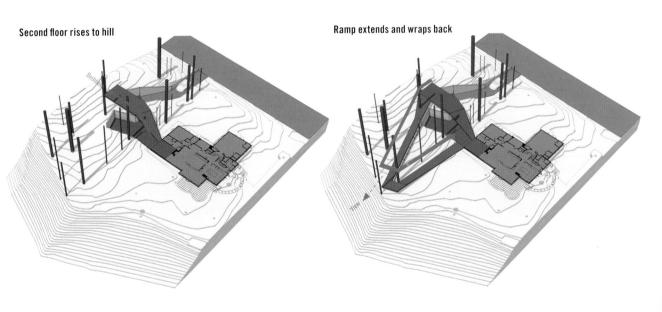

**Second floor rises to hill**

**Ramp extends and wraps back**

In order to engage the ravine (while acknowledging
structural limits), a ramp reaches out from the bedroom
terrace—itself constructed around a mature oak—
to encircle a large tree at the cliff's edge and switches
back to reconnect at the lower level. Enclosing
a triangular moss garden adjoining the gallery,
the ramp completes a circuit that weaves together
interior and exterior, landscape and building.

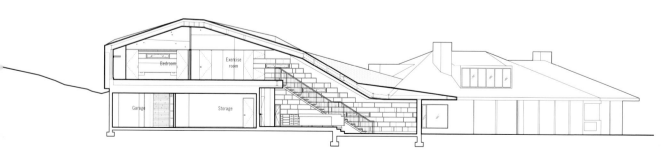

**Section looking north**

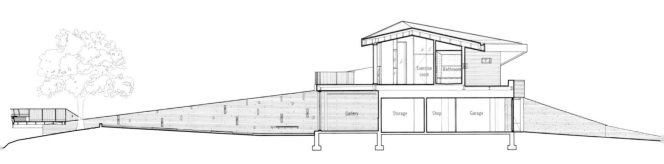

Exercise room  Bathroom

Gallery  Storage  Shop  Garage

Section looking west

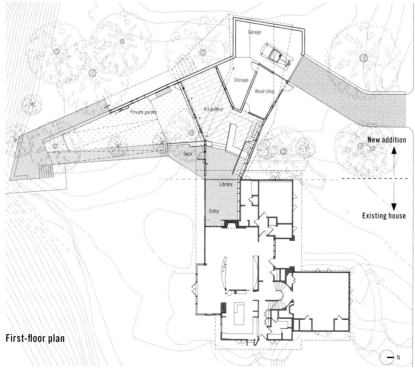

**First-floor plan**

Garage

Storage

Wood shed

Private garden

Art gallery

Deck

Library

Entry

New addition

Existing house

N

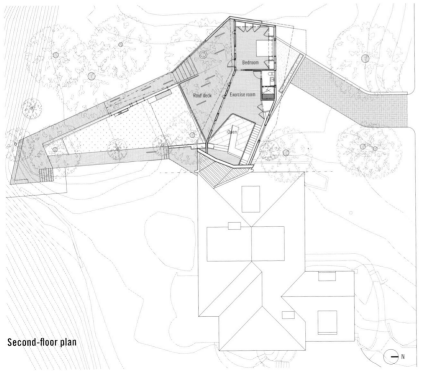

**Second-floor plan**

While the ground-floor spaces are lodged within the mass of the hill, the bedroom floats above the grass-covered rise. A cantilevered stair connects the lower level to the bedroom and terrace above, its treads extending to form a double-height bookcase that links the new and existing portions of the house. Outside, the slate-covered retaining wall runs along the length of the ramp, forming the edge of the moss garden and incorporating lighting, seating, and a stone birdbath.

# Sullivan Family Student Center

Laramie, Wyoming

This project for the University of Wyoming's College of Education transformed two nondescript levels of a recently renovated classroom building into student lounges. The existing conditions consisted of a ring of classrooms around the exterior of the building, leaving only ill-defined open floor areas in the middle. Connected by a central, skylit atrium, the two levels were almost identical, with the exception that the lower floor accommodated the entry vestibule. Dominated by circulation, these spaces lacked the meeting and study areas essential in an educational environment.

The redesign of these zones is based on combining two academic typologies—the picture gallery and the cloister—and exploiting the friction between them. Where the picture gallery is centrifugal, with attention focused outward and movement occurring away from the perimeter walls, the cloister is centripetal, with a circulation zone around the perimeter and attention given to the central courtyard garden. The Sullivan Center is designed as a sequence of concentric zones. The perimeter of the space is lined with a series of photographs about the College of Education mounted to a continuous horizontal stainless steel datum. The corridor is both circulation and a gallery. A custom-milled bamboo plywood screen distinguishes the movement in the gallery/corridor from the stasis in the lounges, while physically linking the two floors and extending around the existing utility core to form a legible, materially specific figure. Apertures in the screen, which range from small slits to full doorways, provide glimpses between the interior lounge and the exterior circulation.

Located in the center of the project, in lieu of the garden in a cloister, is a thirty-four-foot-tall by thirty-foot-wide topographic model of Wyoming, which extends vertically between the two floors. The model is both an abstract sculpted surface, animating the core of the student center, and a highly detailed representation of the contours of the landscape of the state.

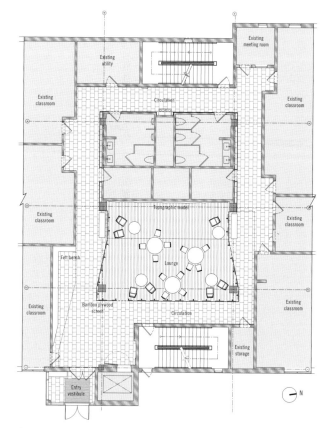

Lower-floor plan

Existing

Upper floor

Lower floor

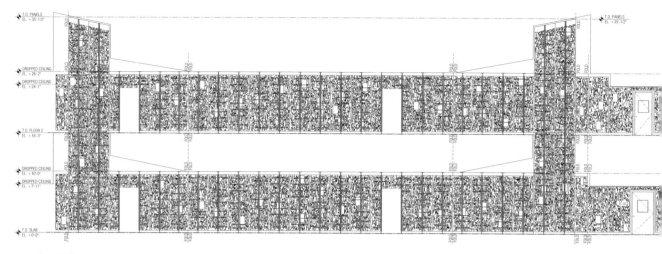

**Unfolded screen**

The milled bamboo plywood screen extends in a continuous band around each floor, and connects vertically between floors in the atrium. The pattern was produced by a computer script that maintained an even amount of porosity across the entire surface, generating a range of aperture sizes and overlaps, and ensuring a nonrepetitive surface that still preserved the screen's structural integrity.

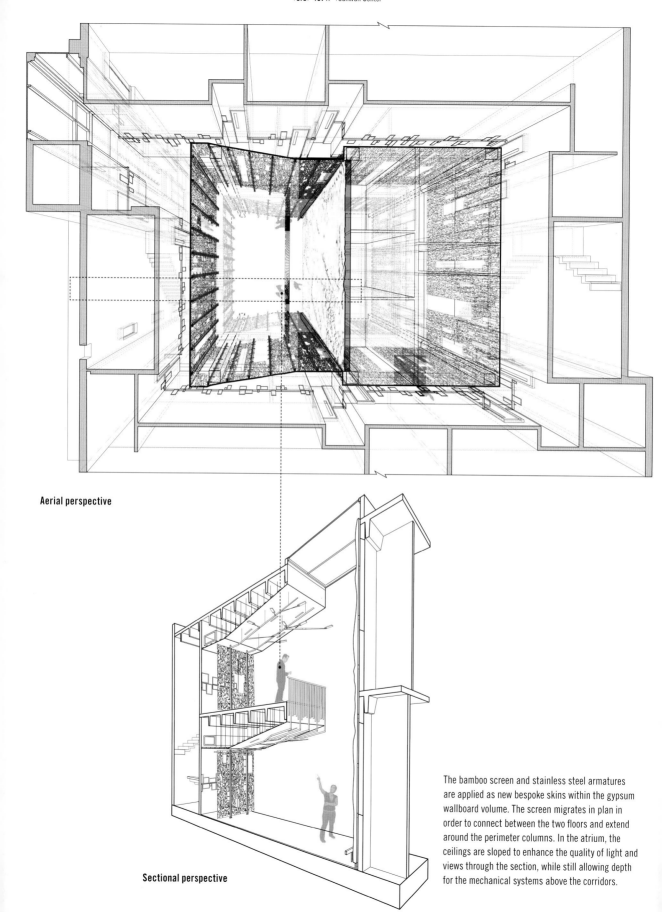

**Aerial perspective**

**Sectional perspective**

The bamboo screen and stainless steel armatures are applied as new bespoke skins within the gypsum wallboard volume. The screen migrates in plan in order to connect between the two floors and extend around the perimeter columns. In the atrium, the ceilings are sloped to enhance the quality of light and views through the section, while still allowing depth for the mechanical systems above the corridors.

Balustrade, ceiling lights, and bamboo screen are integrated into a single unfolding unit. The bamboo is supported by stainless steel armatures, which double as splice plates that are paired with walnut structural posts. The armatures mount to the bamboo at predetermined solid areas in the screen's pattern. Each walnut vertical supports one bamboo panel, with blind splices joining each panel to the next. A horizontal stainless steel chandelier spans between the walnut posts and the balustrade. Resin panels, mounted to torqued steel branches, are positioned as color diffusers under recessed fluorescent fixtures.

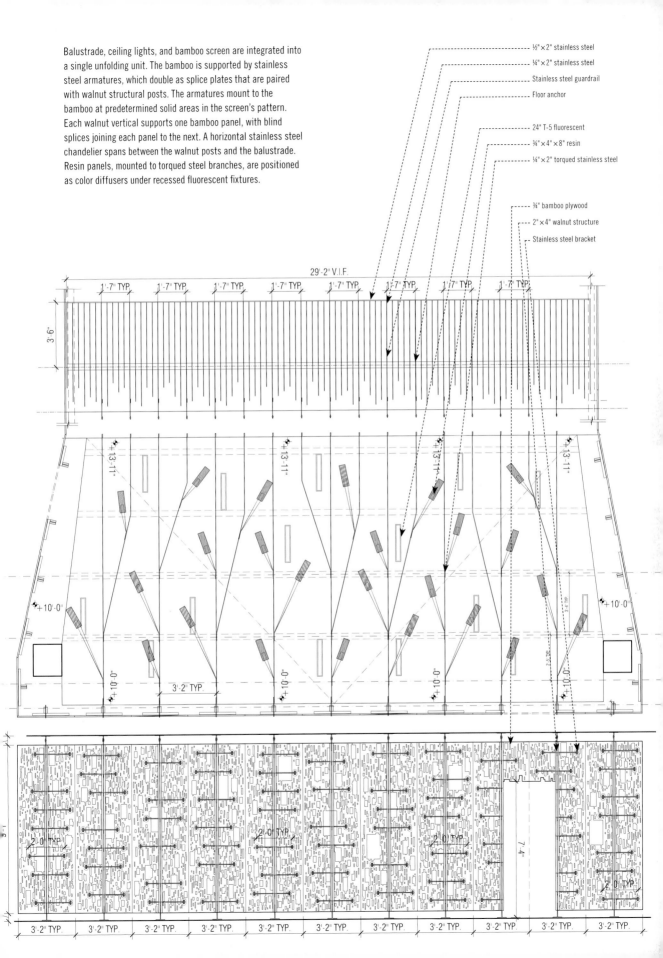

½" × 2" stainless steel

¼" × 2" stainless steel

Stainless steel guardrail

Floor anchor

24" T-5 fluorescent

¾" × 4" × 8" resin

¼" × 2" torqued stainless steel

¾" bamboo plywood

2" × 4" walnut structure

Stainless steel bracket

29'-2" V.I.F.

3'-6"

1'-7" TYP.

+ 13'-11"

+ 10'-0"

3'-2" TYP.

2'-0" TYP.

7'-4"

3'-2" TYP.

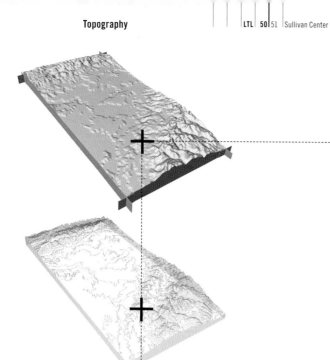

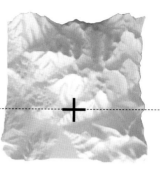

The 1,020-square-foot topographic model of Wyoming is based on contours generated at 200-foot intervals and varies from 1 to 14 inches in thickness. The contour data was converted into a surface with additional details to flesh out the peaks and valleys. The model is rotated clockwise 90 degrees from the conventional position of north up, rendering the model unfamiliar at first glance. More importantly, this aligns the model with actual north in the building and allows sun from the skylight above to more precisely replicate the passage of light across the topography and set to the west of the model.

**Test 7**
.5" ball nose tool, .08" step over
Ranger Board
Accepted: Balanced resolution against cost and time

**Test 5**
.5" ball nose tool, .10" step over
Ultralight medium density fiberboard
Rejected: Raised grain too coarse and variegated

**Test 2**
.125" ball nose tool, .004" step over
Medium density fiberboard
Rejected: Precise resolution but too expensive and slow

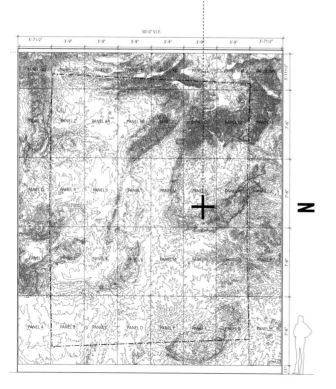

30'-0" V.I.F.

3'-7-1/2"   3'-9"   3'-9"   3'-9"   3'-9"   3'-9"   3'-7-1/2"

**N**

**Test 1**
.125" flat nose tool, .06" step over
Medium density fiberboard
Rejected: Stepped contours lack precision

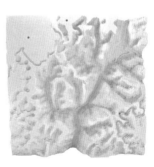

## Installation

Custom steel corner spacers joined the panels and maintained a precise .125" gap. Acrylic epoxy paint was applied as a finished surface.

The panels were more than 14 inches thick in mountainous regions and less than 1 inch thick at the lowest elevations.

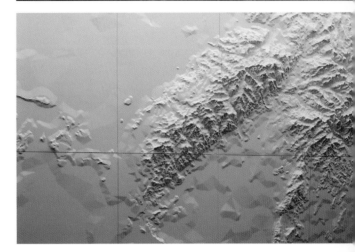

Although the backs of the panels were hollowed out where possible, each one weighed between 100 and 400 pounds.

After receiving a coat of primer paint, the 40 panels were shipped to Wyoming.

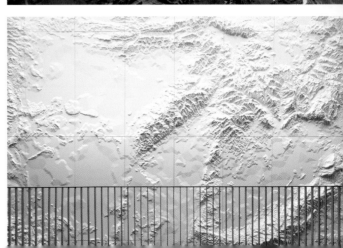

Stacked .75" Ranger Board was milled by Tietz-Baccon in their Long Island City shop.

# Strategic Assessment, Planning and Design

New York, New York

In preparation for its bicentennial year, New York University formed the Office of Strategic Assessment, Planning and Design (SAPD) to oversee the development of the campus environment within the city. The brief for its first physical location mandated an approach that would reflect the elevated design standards of the university while conveying a sense of strict fiscal restraint. The design therefore retained large portions of the previous office build-out and added a single architectural element to accommodate the new program and establish a visual identity for the nascent department. The project centers on maximizing the multivalent performance of this single element: a continuous surface in felt, walnut, and steel. The surface incorporates lighting, acts as a display plane and an acoustical liner, and spatially divides the circulation and office functions. Framing the main conference room opposite the reception desk, the felt surface is immediately visible on entering, defining the public areas of the program while providing continuity throughout the linear space. As it extends from east to west, the surface transforms from vertical to horizontal, becoming sequentially a display counter, pin-up wall, and ceiling plane.

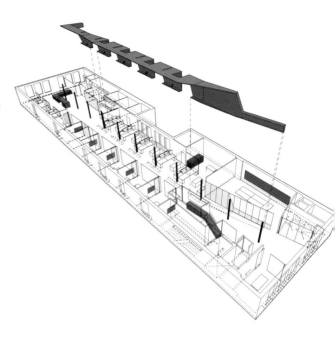

# Spliced Townhouse

New York, New York

This renovation and combination of two apartments occupying several stories of an Upper East Side townhouse derived its design logic from the idiosyncratic sectional condition of the existing architecture. The original nineteenth-century structure had been converted into separate units, a process that resulted in divergent floor levels on the north-facing (street-front) and south-facing (garden) sides of the building. The front of the townhouse retained the original, more expansive heights, whereas the floors added to the southern half resulted in a misalignment of levels among the units being combined. Within a limited square footage (roughly three thousand square feet), the apartment included six distinct floor elevations. The challenge was to reconfigure and integrate these discrete levels and separate units into a single, functioning residence.

Whereas the garden rooms, with their limited ceiling heights, received the private program, the grander spaces on the north facade became the major public rooms, which retained much of the historical detailing and woodwork of the original house and allowed for the display of the owner's collection of contemporary art. The zone between the divergent halves was conceived as a spatial joint or splice, negotiating the multiple elevations and interweaving the public and private circulations. A series of architectural elements was introduced into this gap to stitch the floors together both visually and spatially, thereby reinterpreting and amplifying the vertical format of the typical New York City townhouse.

The primary feature of this interstitial zone is a slatted-wood and blackened-steel screen wrapped by an interconnecting stair. Partly cantilevered and partly suspended, the stair connects the lower-level dining area, formal entry, and living rooms, terminating in a catwalk and mezzanine that form a small library. The stair and screen physically link the different levels of the public program while strategically arranged voids allow for visual transactions between the stacked spaces. On the garden side, a spiral stair encased in a perforated steel cylinder similarly connects the private floors. The continuity of these vertical elements provides coherence to otherwise discontinuous and fragmented spaces.

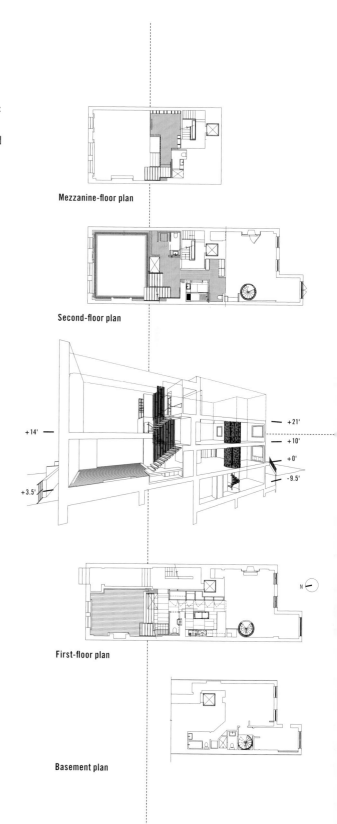

Mezzanine-floor plan

Second-floor plan

First-floor plan

Basement plan

The syncopated rhythm of the oak-and-steel screen produces a shifting experience as one climbs or descends the stair, moving from outside to inside the surface and back again. As it negotiates the five floor heights, the stair incorporates intermediate levels as landings and service programs, implicating the entire house in the experience of vertical movement.

1" × 2 ½" solid walnut board

2 ½" × ½" blackened-steel hanger

¾" × ¾" blackened-steel cross brace

2 ½" × ½" blackened-steel tread support

2" × 12" solid walnut tread

**Second floor**

The garden side of the townhouse incorporates the private program, which includes a new master bedroom and bath, a kitchen, and a guest room. A spiral stair constructed of blackened steel and concrete connects the three private floors and provides a perpendicular contrast to the building's horizontal constraints. Wrapped in a laser-cut cylinder of perforated steel, the spiral stair contrasts in form and materiality with the main stair. As contained as the public stair is expansive, the patterns of the enclosure respond to the varying levels of privacy, shifting from open in the sitting room to dense in the master bedroom above. A rotating, curved-glass panel allows for complete separation of the sleeping quarters when desired.

**First floor**

# Ordos Villa 93

Ordos, Inner Mongolia, China

This project for a villa in Inner Mongolia responds to both the pressures of its unusual geographic site and the social context of the commission. LTL was selected to participate in the Ordos 100 project, choreographed by the artist Ai Weiwei as an elaborate performance piece, for which one hundred architects from around the world were asked to design one hundred villas in one hundred days for a new development galvanized by the arts and located near the regional capital. Each of the houses was to be unique but designed according to a relatively uniform set of parameters: a defined spatial volume on a site within a predetermined master plan. This ambitious experiment incorporated a series of contradictory constraints: the cultural aspirations of the project balanced against the limitations of locally available materials and construction methods; the striking climate of the Gobi Desert, in contrast with the global framework of the commission; and the desire for individual architectural explorations to coexist in close proximity.

 The design for the villa attempts to catalyze these highly specific parameters and to tease out the design opportunities latent in the contradictions. What if the use of available materials and construction techniques could generate spatial and functional distinctions? What if a house could be both introverted and extroverted, combining interiority and exteriority, shelter and exposure, in a single spatial logic? What if the relation between clustered private rooms and open-plan public spaces could be intensified through section? This house seeks a balance between maximizing extensions into the landscape, maintaining intimacy for the owners, and integrating with the closely organized plan of Ordos.

Site: speculation desert

Context: architectural petting zoo

| 100 days |
| :---: |
| + |
| 100 architects |
| + |
| 100 villas |
| + |
| 1,000 m² |

93

Curator: Ai Weiwei

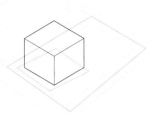

**Given parameters**

**Stretch east-west**

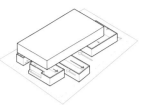

**Capture exterior**

**Link in section**

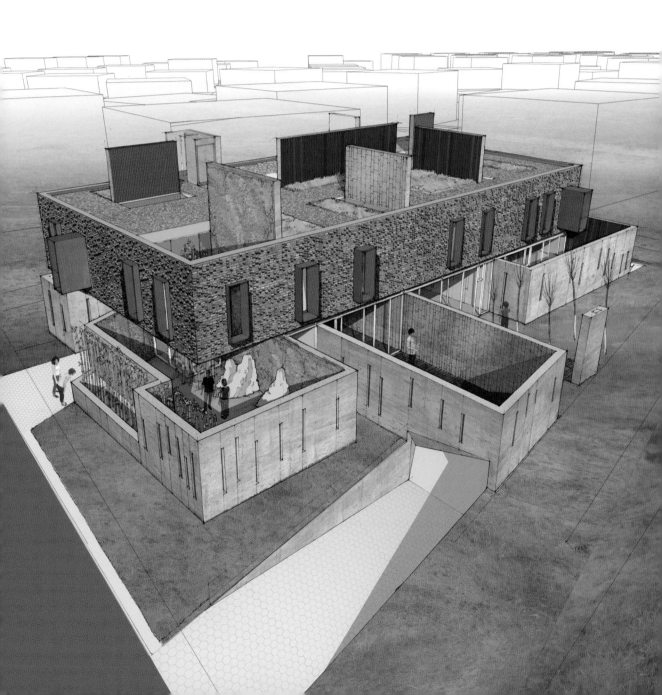

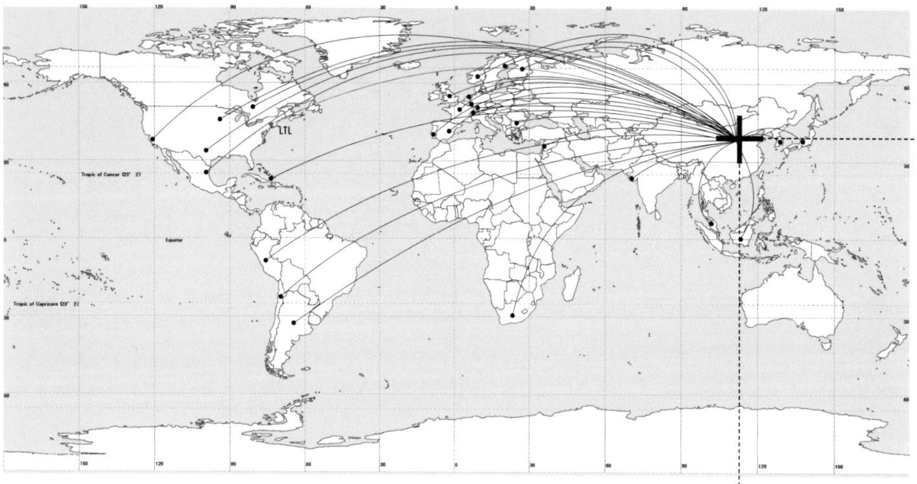

— World

One hundred architecture
firms were selected from
around the globe and
brought together in Inner
Mongolia, China, to work
on the Ordos 100 project.

— China

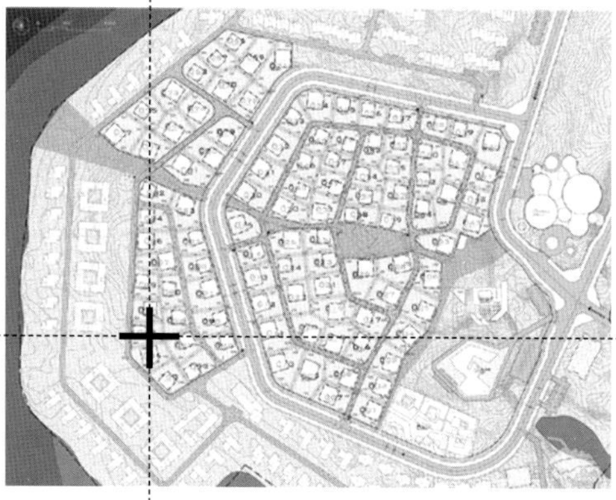

One hundred future
building sites in a new
residential district were
planned around a series
of cultural facilities
to form a community
anchored in the arts.

— Ordos

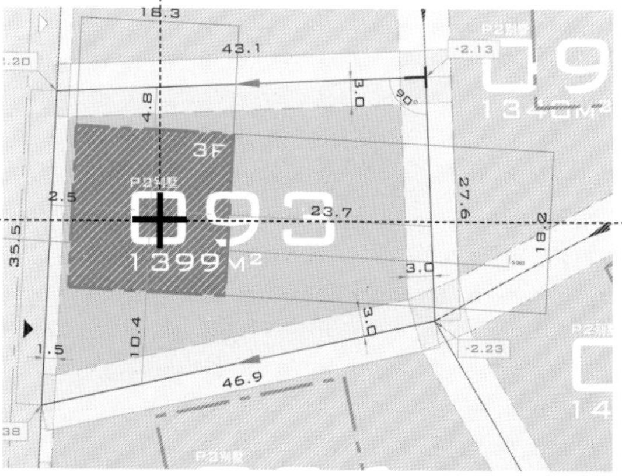

Each architecture firm
selected a site at random
and was given a strict
zoning envelope for a ten
thousand-square-foot villa.

— Site 93

During carefully choreo-graphed and documented site visits, the one hundred architecture firms were taken on police-escorted buses to locate and record the conditions of their selected site. Black is confirmed as the clothing color of choice for architects worldwide.

Blowing silt, dunes, and shrubs on the existing site were in striking contrast to the clarity projected by the zoning maps that informed the site selection and villa number designation.

Site 93 was located, but its lack of permanence and distinguishing characteristics reinforced the contradictions inherent to the project: a site-specific villa for a site without definition.

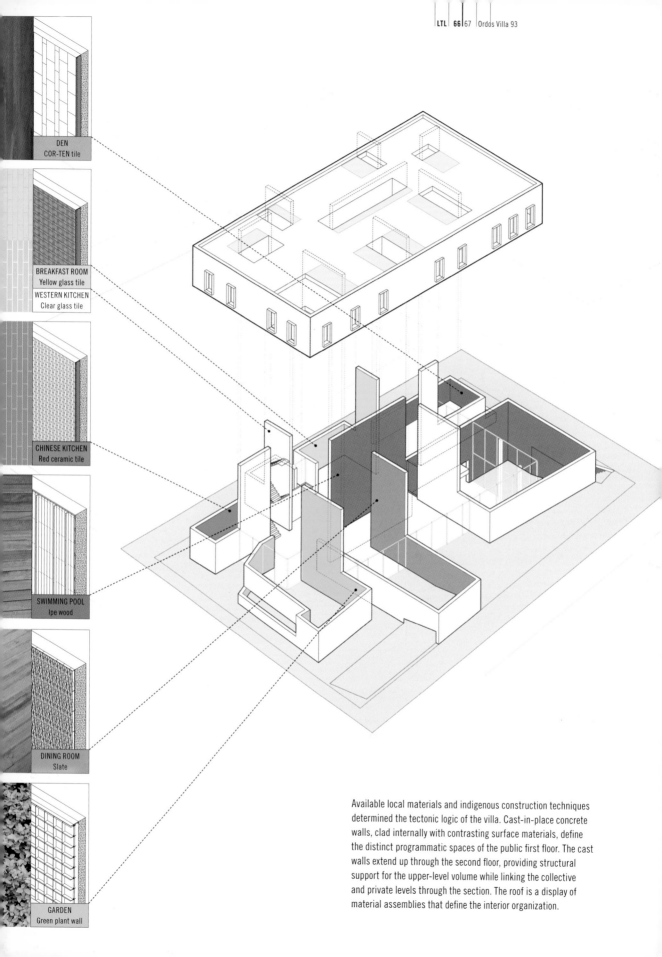

**DEN**
COR-TEN tile

**BREAKFAST ROOM**
Yellow glass tile

**WESTERN KITCHEN**
Clear glass tile

**CHINESE KITCHEN**
Red ceramic tile

**SWIMMING POOL**
Ipe wood

**DINING ROOM**
Slate

**GARDEN**
Green plant wall

Available local materials and indigenous construction techniques determined the tectonic logic of the villa. Cast-in-place concrete walls, clad internally with contrasting surface materials, define the distinct programmatic spaces of the public first floor. The cast walls extend up through the second floor, providing structural support for the upper-level volume while linking the collective and private levels through the section. The roof is a display of material assemblies that define the interior organization.

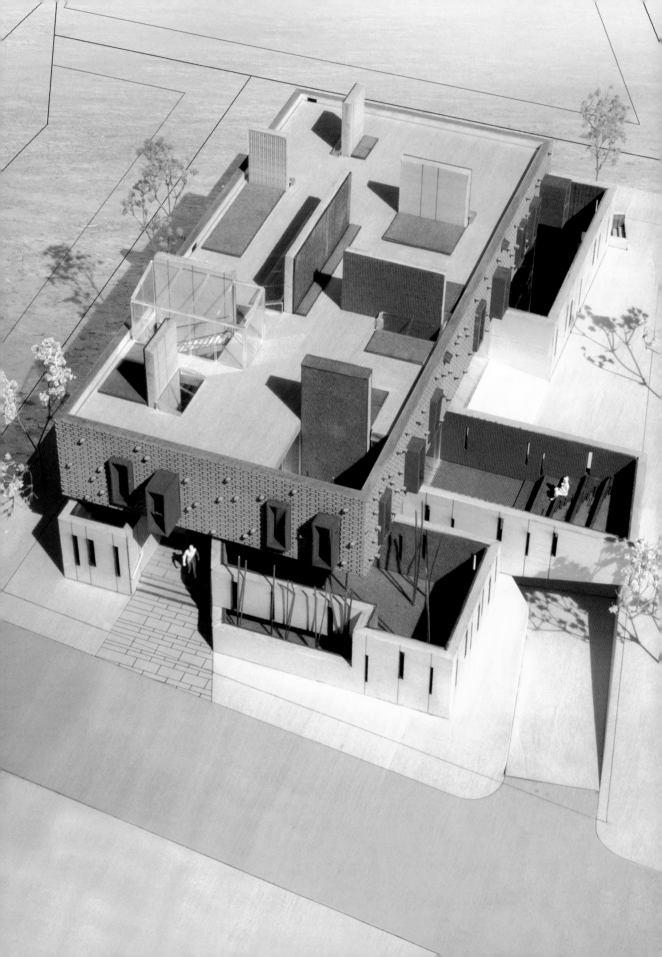

The house is intentionally schizophrenic, extroverted at the ground level and introverted above. A series of wrapping walls, extending from inside to outside and defining both interior and exterior spaces, form the ground plan. For the major public rooms, the walls create courtyards directly linked to specific programs, unfolding the house into the landscape while maintaining privacy and environmental control. In contrast to the open plan of the main floor, the second level comprises an arrangement of enclosed individual rooms, including a master suite to the east.

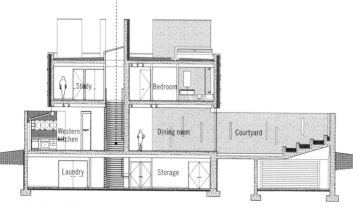

**Section looking east**

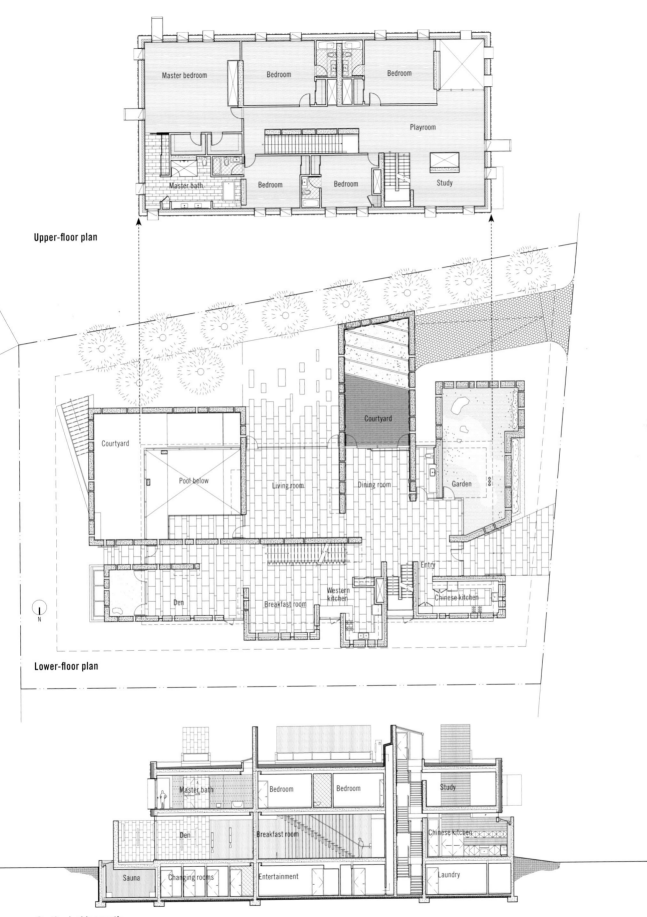

**Upper-floor plan**

Master bedroom

Bedroom

Bedroom

Playroom

Master bath

Bedroom

Bedroom

Study

**Lower-floor plan**

N

Courtyard

Courtyard

Pool below

Living room

Dining room

Garden

Den

Breakfast room

Western kitchen

Entry

Chinese kitchen

**Section looking south**

Master bath

Bedroom

Bedroom

Study

Den

Breakfast room

Chinese kitchen

Sauna

Changing rooms

Entertainment

Laundry

The two main volumes of the house are separated by a horizontal sliver of glass that rings the entire structure, creating the illusion that the solid mass of the second floor is hovering above the courtyard walls at the main level.

The private second level is defined as a single mass, clad in a modified Flemish-bond of local gray brick to reinforce its solidity. Door-size windows punch through this exterior surface and are wrapped in COR-TEN steel frames that extend to form private balconies.

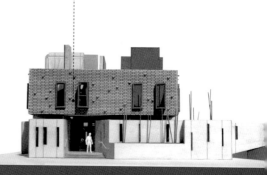

**North**

**West**

The swimming pool is located in the lowest level of the villa, carved into the terrain of the site. Views toward the sky are captured in the gap between the ceiling and the outer walls of an excavated courtyard.

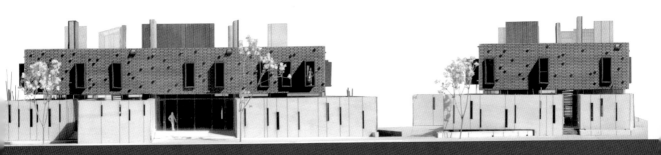

South

East

# The Open Planning Project

New York, New York

The design for the office and meeting space of the Open Planning Project directly engages the nonprofit group's mission: advocacy for public access to urban space. In addition to the variety of conference rooms, meeting spaces, and pantry areas that foster open interaction among members, LTL designed a central, democratic shared work space at the heart of the project. Linear desks of bamboo enable flexible and easy exchange between employees. A large, built-in walnut bookshelf doubles as a 1:450 scaled map of Manhattan. The map shelf anchors the main space as an accessible repository for the wide range of publications on urban policy and planning, the collection of maps and globes, and the living green wall that represents Central Park.

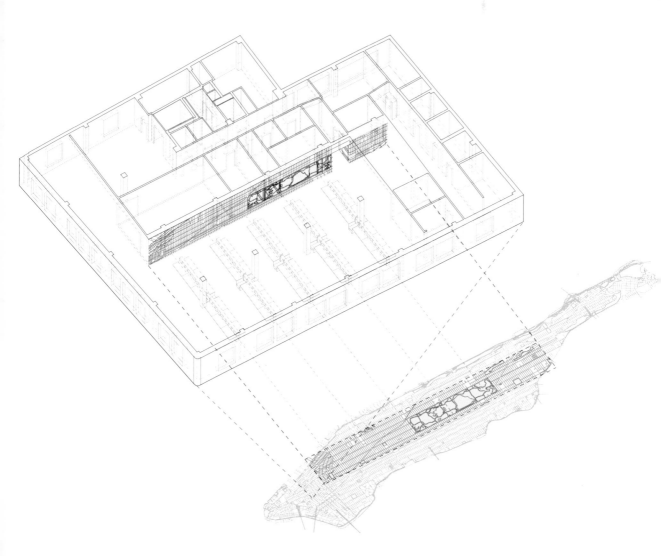

The feature bookshelf wall maps the mission of the client: Blocks of Manhattan house information, streets of various sizes and orientations form shelving divisions, and public parks are green and grow.

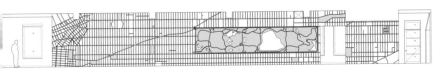

# New Taipei City Museum of Art

New Taipei City, Taiwan

Whereas conventional art museums are designed to distinguish and elevate art from the everyday, this competition entry for the New Taipei City (NTC) Museum of Art seamlessly integrates public life with the experience of art. A resolution of simultaneous opposites, the museum is at once an object building—a logical response to the limitations of site coverage—and an extension into the landscape. As an iconic volume floating over an open plaza, the program is consolidated into a single identifiable prism; the terrain below is at the same time sculpted to engage the multiple approaches and points of vehicular and pedestrian access to the site. As the landscape flows under the building, the ceramic skin stretches from the central mass across the adjacent park into a horizontal shading device, providing refuge from sun and rain and marking the entries and circulation routes into the museum.

A continuous lobby, containing a grand staircase and pairs of escalators, spirals up through the eight floors of the building. The stairs extend into public gathering spaces at each level and link to the central elevator core, which provides a means to short-circuit the spiraling ascent. Filled with art that mixes with the crowds moving through the building, this dynamic space gathers a multitude of programs, including café, retail, exhibition, and library. Ascending the public spiral, one can access the more discrete galleries and, through choreographed views, look out on the unfolding panorama of the city and landscape. Exuberant, constantly changing, and complex in section, the continuous lobby forms a legible figure in plan. The various galleries and program areas, on each floor organized around this recognizable core, are more functional and straightforward, providing a neutral backdrop to the exhibitions and activities they host.

Program = 51,052 m²

Raise program above a porous plinth

Contour the porous plinth

Continuous lobby through program

The NTC Museum of Art comprises a faceted cubic volume surmounting an open public plinth. Whereas the volume consolidates the primary museum program into a vertically stacked sequence, the plinth engages the public park, extending horizontally into the surrounding landscape. The museum volume is organized internally by a continuous spiral lobby and wrapped by an external skin of ceramic fins. The prismatic volume, with its subtly distorted shape, presents a varying profile at every side, changing relative to the position of the observer into a subtle and shifting silhouette.

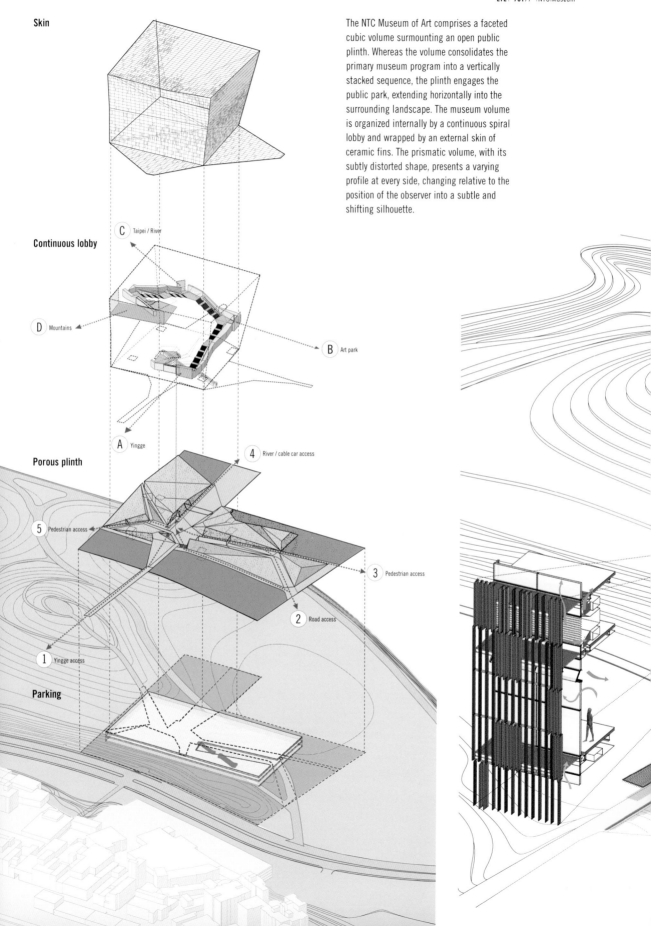

**Skin**

**Continuous lobby**

C  Taipei / River

D  Mountains

B  Art park

A  Yingge

**Porous plinth**

4  River / cable car access

5  Pedestrian access

3  Pedestrian access

2  Road access

1  Yingge access

**Parking**

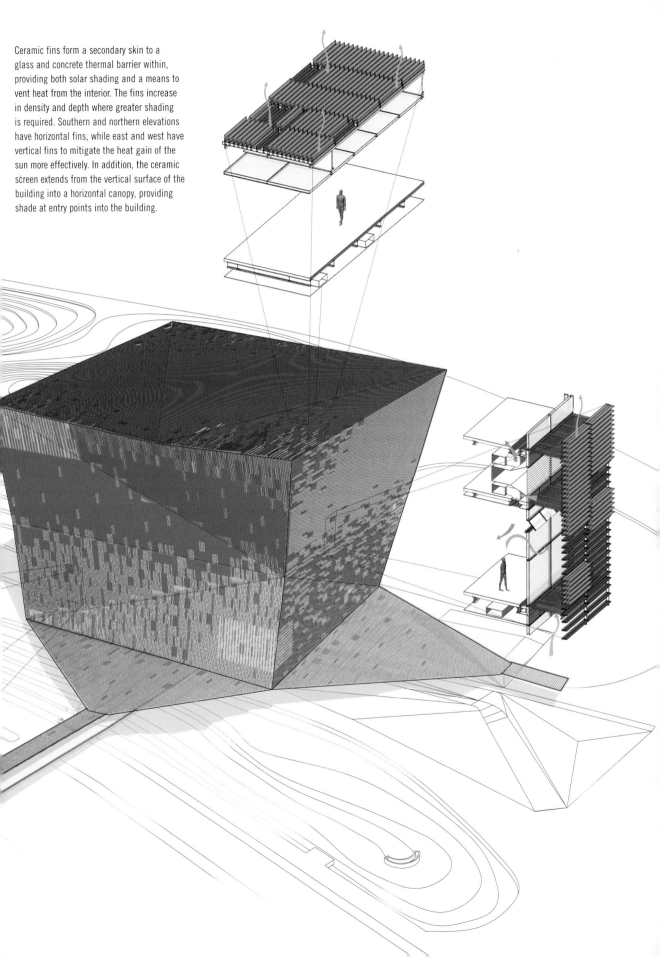

Ceramic fins form a secondary skin to a glass and concrete thermal barrier within, providing both solar shading and a means to vent heat from the interior. The fins increase in density and depth where greater shading is required. Southern and northern elevations have horizontal fins, while east and west have vertical fins to mitigate the heat gain of the sun more effectively. In addition, the ceramic screen extends from the vertical surface of the building into a horizontal canopy, providing shade at entry points into the building.

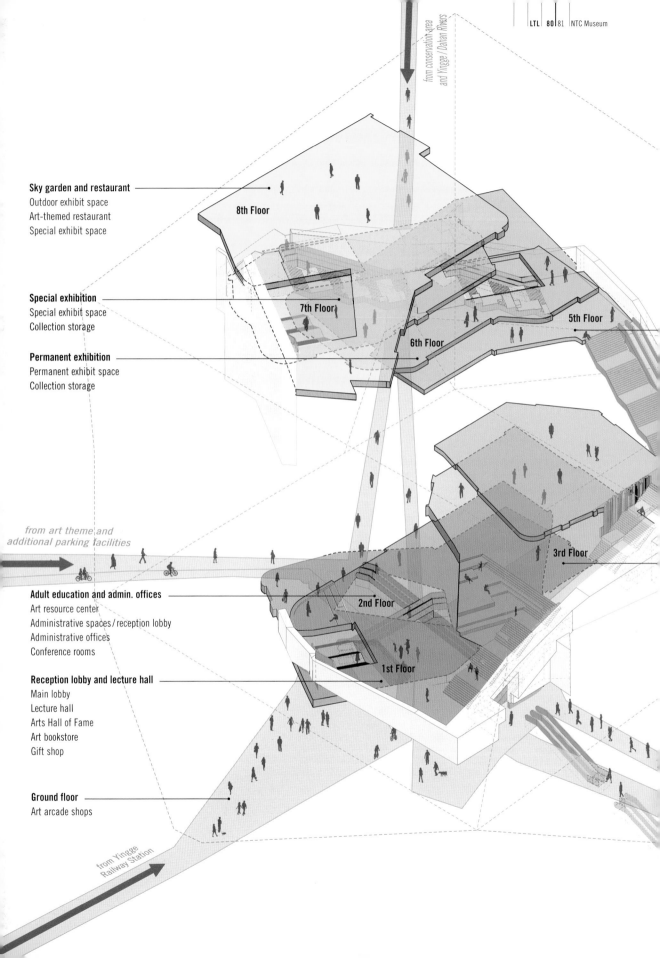

from conservation area
and Yingge / Dahan Rivers

**Sky garden and restaurant**
Outdoor exhibit space
Art-themed restaurant
Special exhibit space

8th Floor

**Special exhibition**
Special exhibit space
Collection storage

7th Floor

5th Floor

6th Floor

**Permanent exhibition**
Permanent exhibit space
Collection storage

3rd Floor

from art theme and
additional parking facilities

**Adult education and admin. offices**
Art resource center
Administrative spaces / reception lobby
Administrative offices
Conference rooms

2nd Floor

1st Floor

**Reception lobby and lecture hall**
Main lobby
Lecture hall
Arts Hall of Fame
Art bookstore
Gift shop

**Ground floor**
Art arcade shops

from Yingge
Railway Station

**Eighth floor**

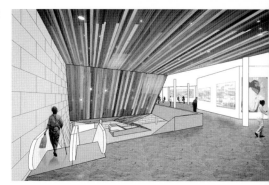

**Sixth floor**

from ceramic park and future
transportation facilities

**Permanent exhibition**
Permanent exhibit space
Collection storage

**Fifth floor**

**Children's education**
Resource center, children's education
Art classrooms
Audiovisual room

**Children's exhibition and admin. offices**
Children's Museum of Art main lobby
Special exhibit space, children's arts
Administrative lobby
Administrative offices
Conference rooms

**Third floor**

**First floor**

from tour bus
surface parking

asement
king

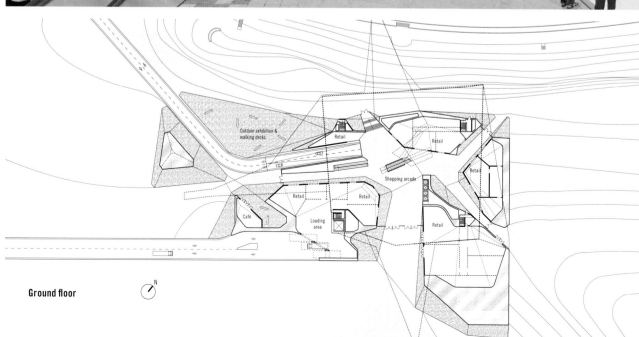

**Ground floor**

N

Outdoor exhibition & walking decks

Retail

Retail

Shopping arcade

Retail

Retail

Retail

Café

Loading area

Retail

The continuous lobby spirals through all eight levels of the NTC Museum of Art, punctuated by choreographed views of the city, the mountains, and the Dahan River. The experience of the collective space oscillates between the art and activities within and the surrounding environmental context. The stair itself acts as a complex landscape that adapts and responds to program and use. Extending at each floor level to become terraced seating, display, and furniture, the stair is a space of inhabitation as well as circulation.

Acting as an inversion of the traditional raised podium, the porous plinth allows the surrounding park landscape to extend beneath the main mass of the museum. Incorporating entry, retail, and exhibition, this public plaza provides a dynamic terrain for both commerce and art, engaging the multiple access points and circulations into the site. Escalators rise through a faceted domelike ceiling into the museum volume, initiating an ascent from ground to sky.

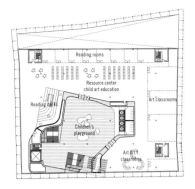

**Fourth floor**

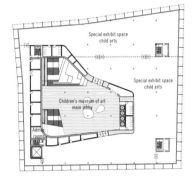

**Third floor**

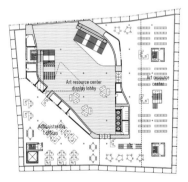

**Second floor**

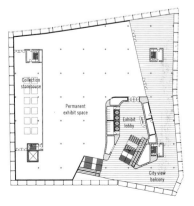

**First floor**

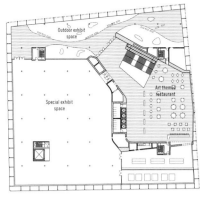

**Eighth floor**

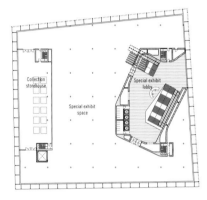

**Seventh floor**

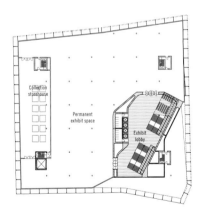

**Sixth floor**

**Fifth floor**

# New New York
## Fast Forward

Architectural League of New York, New York

This exhibition, organized by the Architectural League of New York, took stock of the significant developments in architecture and planning in New York City during the height of the construction boom in the spring of 2007. More than six hundred new building or planning projects, either under construction or in design, were mapped onto individual cards located at eye level atop steel posts. The cards were placed around the perimeter of a map of New York City's five boroughs and each was connected by a red string to its corresponding location on the map, which was rendered on a large table and anamorphically stretched to fit within the room. The new projects engulfed the map, while the varying density of red indicated the wide-ranging concentrations and locations of building activity within the city. In the adjacent gallery, three additional maps described unique sites where extensive development was under way. Video interviews with thirty New York–based architects discussing critical issues related to the ongoing transformation of the city and its built environment played on monitors located around the gallery perimeter.

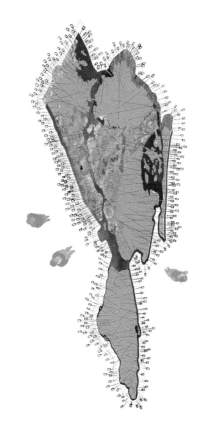

# MSK Lobby Wall

New York, New York

The lobby of Memorial Sloan-Kettering Cancer Center's new Zuckerman Research Center anticipated a feature art wall as a central component of the active entry space connecting Sixty-Eighth and Sixty-Ninth Streets on the Upper East Side of New York City. LTL's approach challenged the premise of standard lobby sculpture, work that is euphemistically described as "plop art" to connote its lack of site-specific connectivity. In this case, LTL designed a piece that would at once visually seduce and reflect back the activity of the lobby. In keeping with the given lobby design, the sculpture began as a solid wall, three feet six inches deep, thirty feet wide, and twelve feet six inches tall. Emanating from station points mapped in plan and section and identifying the typical locations of human activity within the lobby, 230 vision cones were projected into the wall, creating conical intersections. These cones are controlled by a regular grid on the side of the wall that faces the main lobby area, and they exit the back of the wall in a seemingly random collection of variously sized ellipses. As users of the lobby move around the sculpture, conical alignments embedded in the wall become visible, identifying 230 precise source locations throughout the lobby. The experience is designed to intensify the public, social aspects of the space.

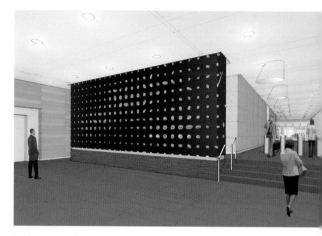

Lobby perspective

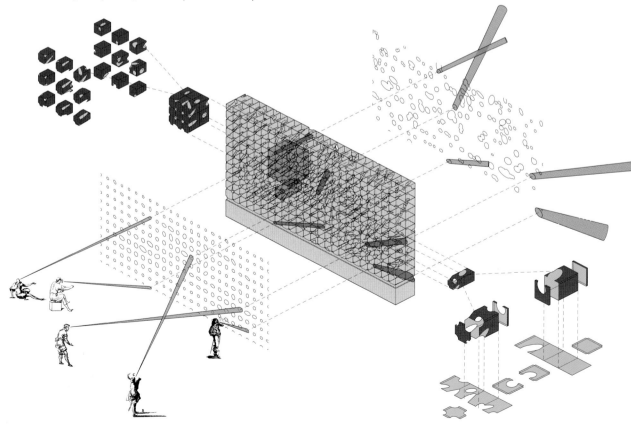

The lobby wall realizes the tension between the rational and the random: The logical process required to project 230 vision cones through the 528 boxes on one side of the wall contrasts with the seemingly haphazard arrangement of elliptical voids on the other side.

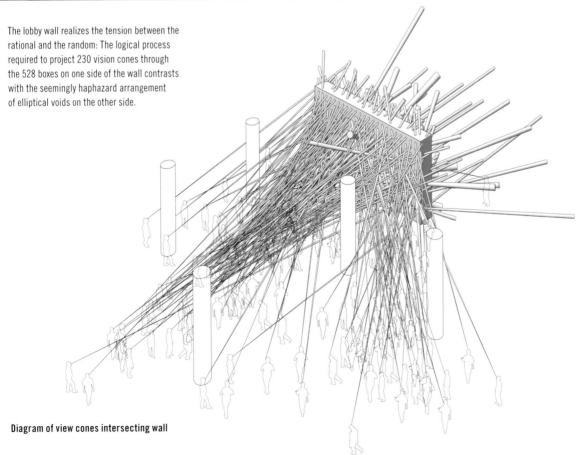

**Diagram of view cones intersecting wall**

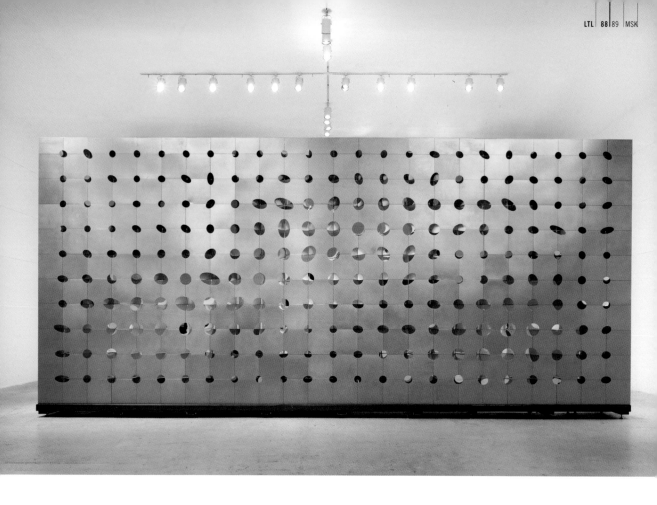

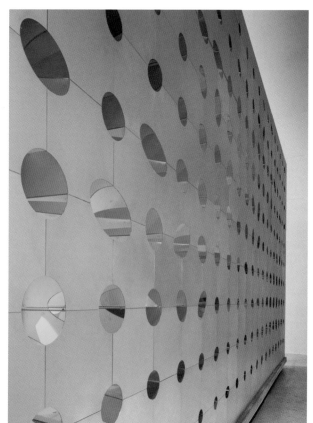

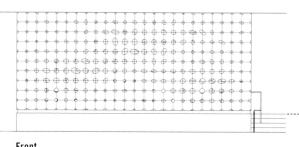

**Front**

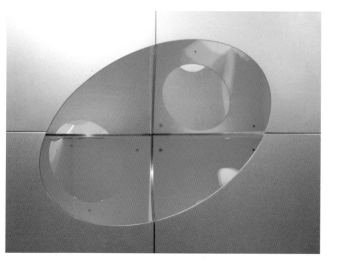

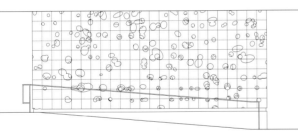

**Back**

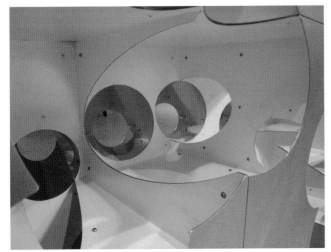

Prior to fabrication, LTL examined the digital design of the project by closely inspecting the 3,168 individual surfaces of the 528 boxes. This test qualified the initial assumptions of the digital model and identified a range of potential complications, from unsupported sides to fragments floating in digital suspension. For each potentially deficient box, the conical source was adjusted and the digital model re-intersected, and then evaluated for its conformity to physical fabrication requirements. Each adjustment impacted other boxes, however, resulting in a complicated, multistage redesign and verification process.

 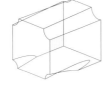 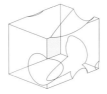  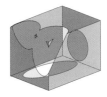

Type 1: good     Type 2: OK, two sides supported     Type 3: fair, weak corner     Type 4: bad, one-side weld     Type 5: reject, floating fragment

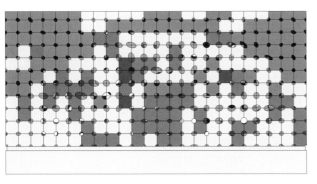 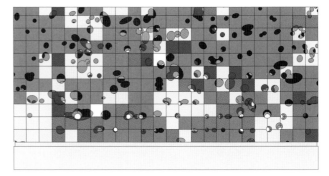

**Front**     **Back**

In addition to analyzing the structural solidity of the boxes, LTL tested the lobby wall to meet other performance requirements for translating from digital design to physical production. Moving from Rhino surface modeling to SolidWorks objects introduced material dimensions to the model, further complicating the legibility of the conical intersections. Assembly sequence required the inclusion of hidden apertures to boxes not yet accessible by the human hand.

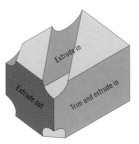 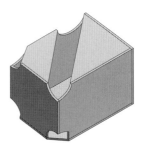

Rhino surface box     SolidWorks composite

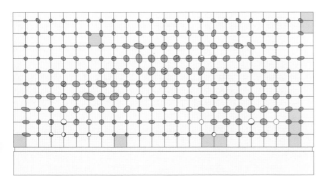 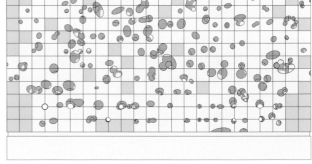

**Identification of boxes requiring concealed access holes for assembly**

**Laser-cutting 3168 sides:** LTL worked closely with the Philadelphia-based metal designers and fabricators Veyko to determine the stainless-steel welding, finishing, and assembly system for realizing the piece. Veyko translated the Rhino-based model into SolidWorks in order to precisely cut the 3,168 custom pieces that would form the sides of the boxes.

**Welding 1.67 linear miles:** To meet the high level of precision necessary for the project, Veyko constructed a custom welding jig out of aluminum to absorb the heat from the stainless steel continuous linear welds. After five of the six sides of a given box had been joined, a hydraulic piston pushed the box off the jig, which would have shrunk during cooling. In total, 8,856 linear feet of continuous welds were laid.

**Finishing 528 boxes:** When each box was completed, its welds were ground smooth. The interior was then finished with a highly reflective, fluorescent-yellow matte powder coat to allow the maximum amount of ambient light to bounce throughout the interior. For the exterior stainless-steel surfaces, Veyko customized a contrasting bead-blasted finish that would not show fingerprints.

**Assembling one lobby wall:** Each individually welded box was mechanically fastened to all the adjacent boxes, creating a monolithic, self-structuring wall. To rehearse the assembly sequence and verify tolerances prior to installation in Memorial Sloan-Kettering, the wall was test-assembled in a gallery in Philadelphia.

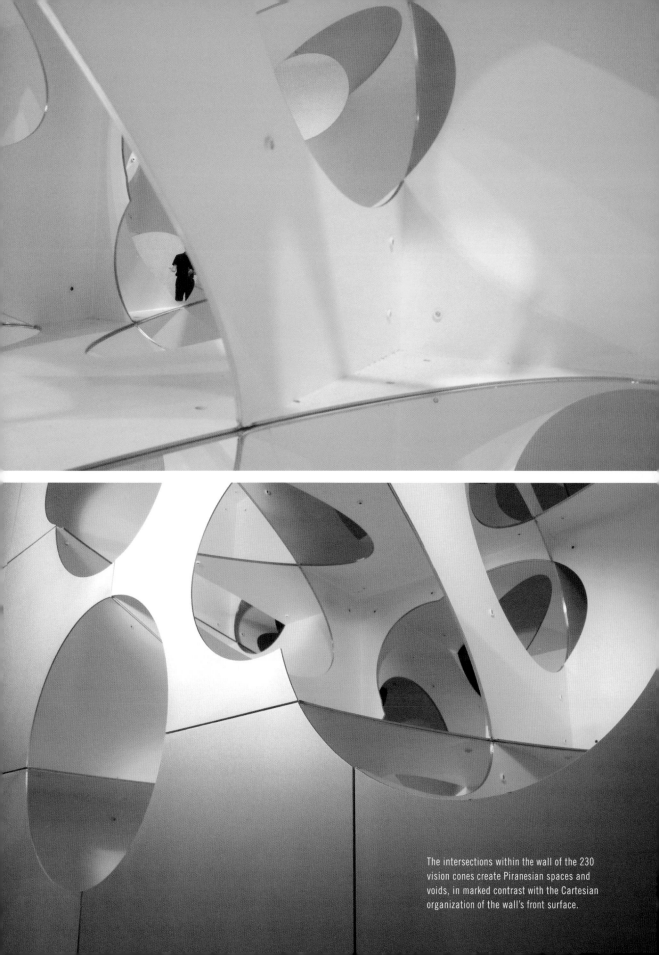

The intersections within the wall of the 230 vision cones create Piranesian spaces and voids, in marked contrast with the Cartesian organization of the wall's front surface.

# Living and Learning Residence Hall 6

Gallaudet University, Washington, DC

In the fall of 2010, LTL, in collaboration with Quinn Evans Architects and SIGAL Construction, won the commission for a residential and educational center on the Gallaudet University campus, known as the Living and Learning Residence Hall 6 (LLRH6). As the only liberal arts university dedicated to the education of deaf and hard-of-hearing individuals, Gallaudet wanted to create an exemplary building tailored to deaf, cognitive, linguistic, and cultural ways of being. LTL worked closely with representatives of the school to incorporate the challenges and opportunities of DeafSpace design principles. These guidelines were developed by the university's ASL and Deaf Studies Department, under the direction of the architect Hansel Bauman, to formulate spatial logics that support clear visual communication through sign language and enhance visual and tactile spatial awareness. In expanding the residential program to include public gathering spaces and in locating the hall directly on the historic mall, Gallaudet sought to change the current separation between the residential and academic components of the campus, reactivating the mall as the center of vibrant university life.

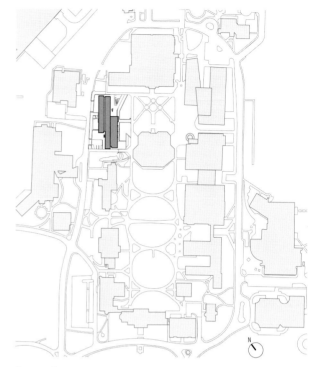

**Campus plan**

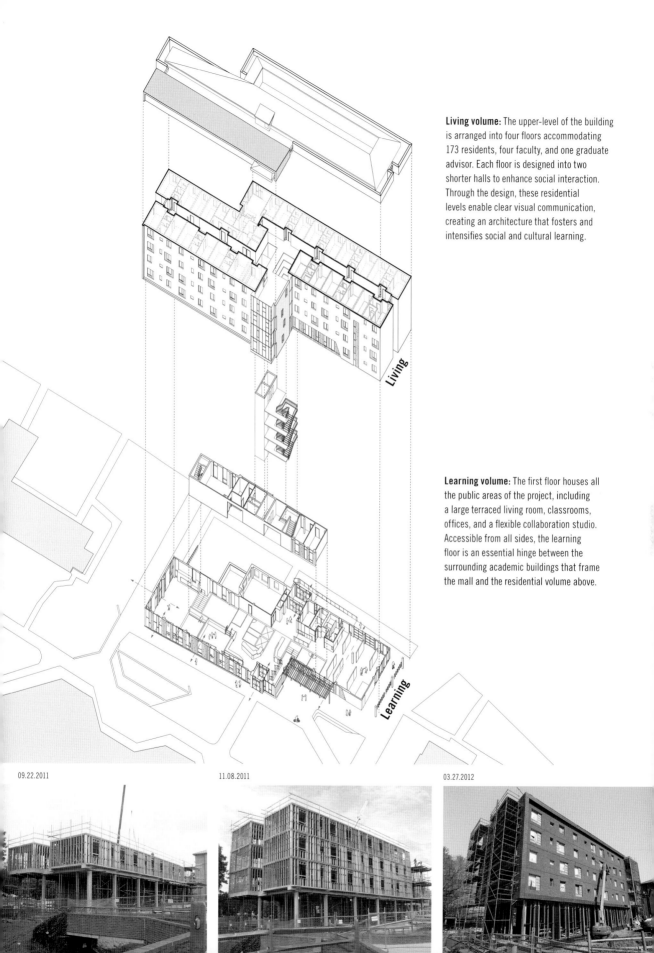

**Living volume:** The upper-level of the building is arranged into four floors accommodating 173 residents, four faculty, and one graduate advisor. Each floor is designed into two shorter halls to enhance social interaction. Through the design, these residential levels enable clear visual communication, creating an architecture that fosters and intensifies social and cultural learning.

Living

**Learning volume:** The first floor houses all the public areas of the project, including a large terraced living room, classrooms, offices, and a flexible collaboration studio. Accessible from all sides, the learning floor is an essential hinge between the surrounding academic buildings that frame the mall and the residential volume above.

Learning

09.22.2011                    11.08.2011                    03.27.2012

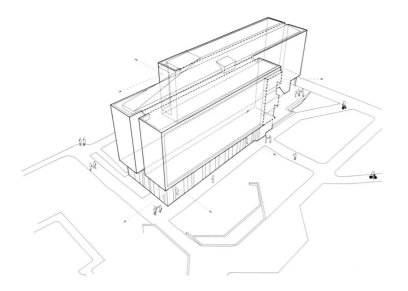

**Sensory reach**: The design amplifies and extends visual means of deaf communication within the building and between interior and exterior spaces. Extensive use of glass opens the public spaces of the first floor to the campus grounds, while vertically stacked lounges and faculty apartments on the two sides of the building provide visual anchors from afar. The legible three-bar diagram of the architecture establishes the basis for clear paths of circulation and a recognizable spatial organization for residents and visitors.

09.22.2011

11.08.2011

03.27.2012

**Proximity of bodies:** The design of the first floor uses DeafSpace concepts of "proximics of communication"—the distance relationship of bodies, both near and far to create a multilayered space. The plan simultaneously establishes clear lines of sight, enabling the user to quickly determine the overall orientation from all entrances, while providing smaller, distinct, terraced areas and rooms for more intimate exchanges and groupings.

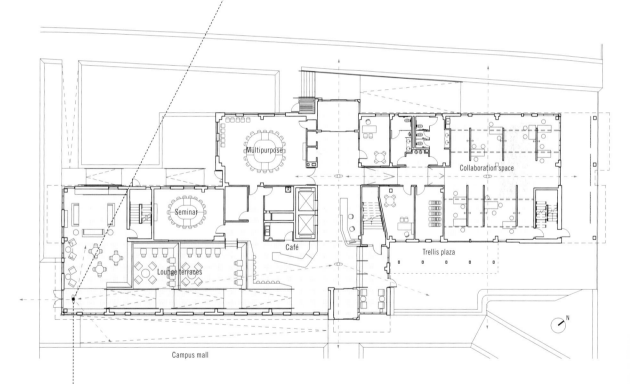

Multipurpose

Collaboration space

Seminar

Café

Trellis plaza

Lounge terraces

Campus mall

N

05.04.2012

**Color and light definition**: At the core of DeafSpace principles is the desire to create an architecture that enables communication through sign language. LTL's design for LLRH6 deploys wide hallways with adjacent niches at the entrance to each residential suite, providing the additional space needed for conversation in sign language. The design of the open central staircase creates sectional gaps and openings that intensify multiple lines of exchange between the four residential floors.

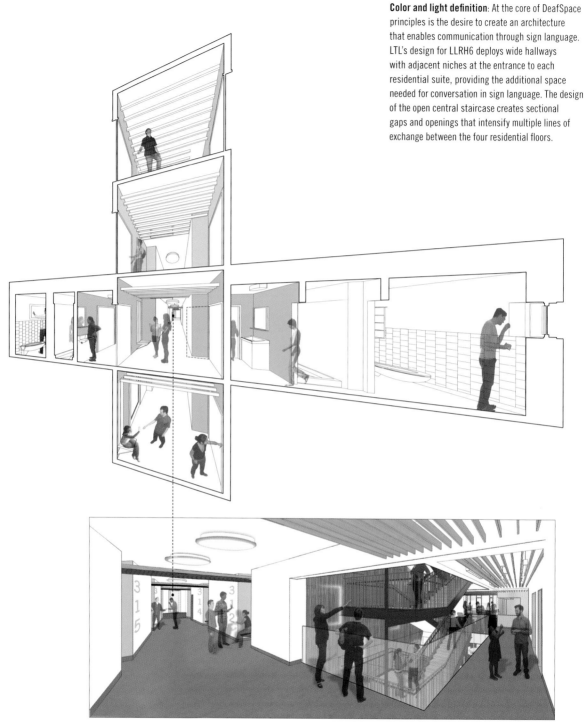

05.04.2012

**Mobility and visual control**: DeafSpace principles emphasize the appropriate application of light and color to enable clear visual communication while alleviating eye strain. The judicious use of distinctive colors mitigates high levels of contrast while establishing identifiable codes for each floor. A four-story feature wall, articulated through concealed lights, highlights the main communicating staircase that links to lounges and full kitchens, thus establishing the collective center for fostering events and conversation.

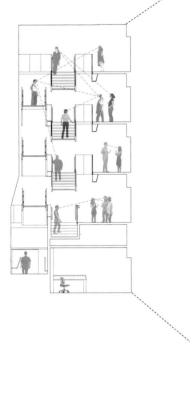

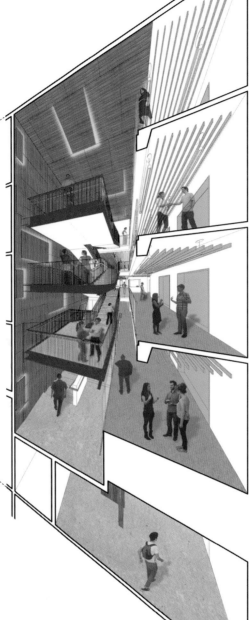

11.08.2011

03.07.2012

04.05.2012

# The Grid and the Superblock

New York, New York

The Commissioner's Plan of 1811 established
the grid as the principal ordering mechanism for the
speculative territory of Manhattan. The regularity
and homogeneity of its 2,028 proposed blocks was a
limiting device that has generally prevented the imposi-
tion of larger, more dominant systems, ensuring an
ease of vehicular and pedestrian flow that aerates the
density of the city. Where this system breaks down,
pathologies develop in the local urban tissue, and the
social vigor that typifies New York street life is subject
to retardation and stagnation.

This proposal for the Hudson Square
district contends with precisely such a disruption in
the Manhattan grid. Hudson Square exists at the
edge of three of the city's most vibrant historic and
developing neighborhoods: the West Village to the north,
Soho to the east, and Tribeca to the south. To the
west is the newly developed landscape of Hudson River
Park and Pier 40, along with desirable views of the
Hudson River across the West Side Highway. While the
site is relatively porous along its northern and eastern
edges, the grid in Hudson Square is interrupted by two
multiblock structures: the UPS facility and St. John's
Center. Together the two buildings produce a massive
obstacle to east-west movement and sever any meaningful connection to the river and the park.

Recognizing that these two monoliths are
likely to remain for economic and logistical reasons, this
project reimagines and exploits these apparent impedi-
ments in order to produce a new form of metropolitan
sectional density. A series of stacked and interconnected
layers combines housing, park space, and commer-
cial and retail activity in a dynamic mix. The proposal
asks: Can the very idiosyncrasies of these anomalous
structures sponsor an unprecedented urbanism that rec-
onciles the logic of the grid with the expansive territory
of the superblock?

UPS facility

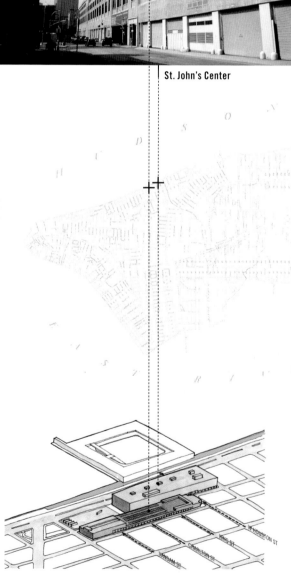

St. John's Center

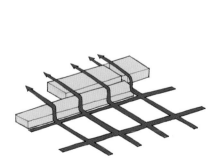

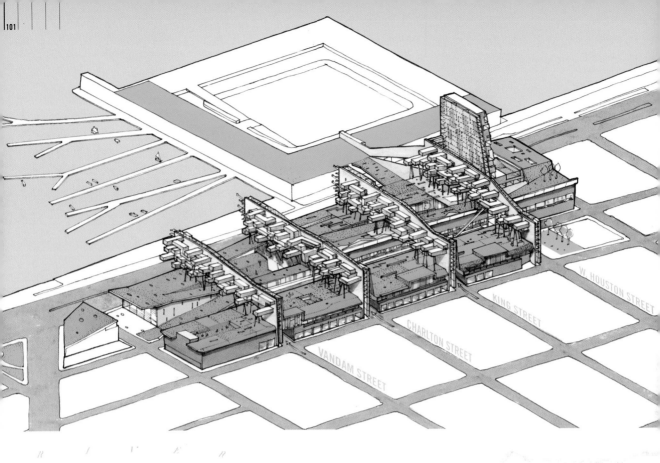

**Raise Washington Street:** Recognizing that Washington Street is dominated at ground level by the operations of UPS and the new Department of Sanitation garage, this proposal elevates the primary flow of traffic one full story, reinstating the north-south automotive passage and creating the possibility of a more active retail avenue, freed from the industrial activity below.

**Green the superblock:** The vast roof surfaces of the superblocks are reimagined as inhabitable landscapes. Developed to take advantage of the extreme length of the buildings, the roofscapes accommodate linear activity—swimming pools, running tracks, and pedestrian walks—while they register the geometry of the grid through a series of differentiated planting zones. Providing needed park space and urban gardens to the surrounding neighborhood, the planted surfaces absorb runoff, insulate the superblocks, and mitigate the pollution associated with the nearby Holland Tunnel.

**Extend the sidewalk:** The four-block UPS facility is opened strategically at the terminus of the east-west street grid, drawing King, Charlton, and Vandam Streets through the building to the elevated Washington Street. The sidewalk is stretched into a diagonal ribbon that extends above the roofs of the superblocks to provide circulation for a system of housing units. A series of five-story walls furnishes structural and infrastructural support to the housing cantilevered over the rooftop park.

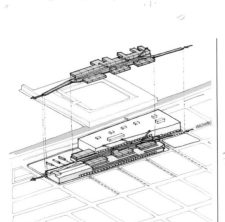

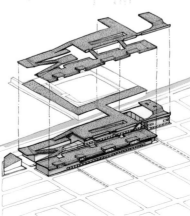

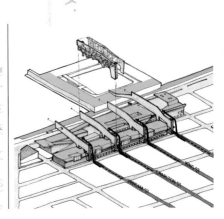

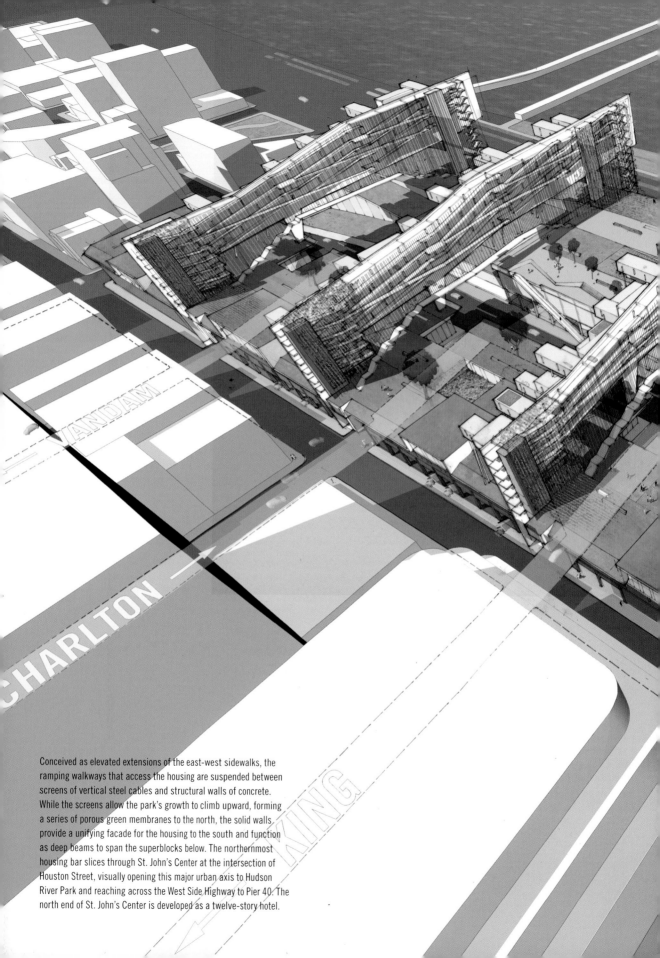

Conceived as elevated extensions of the east-west sidewalks, the ramping walkways that access the housing are suspended between screens of vertical steel cables and structural walls of concrete. While the screens allow the park's growth to climb upward, forming a series of porous green membranes to the north, the solid walls provide a unifying facade for the housing to the south and function as deep beams to span the superblocks below. The northernmost housing bar slices through St. John's Center at the intersection of Houston Street, visually opening this major urban axis to Hudson River Park and reaching across the West Side Highway to Pier 40. The north end of St. John's Center is developed as a twelve-story hotel.

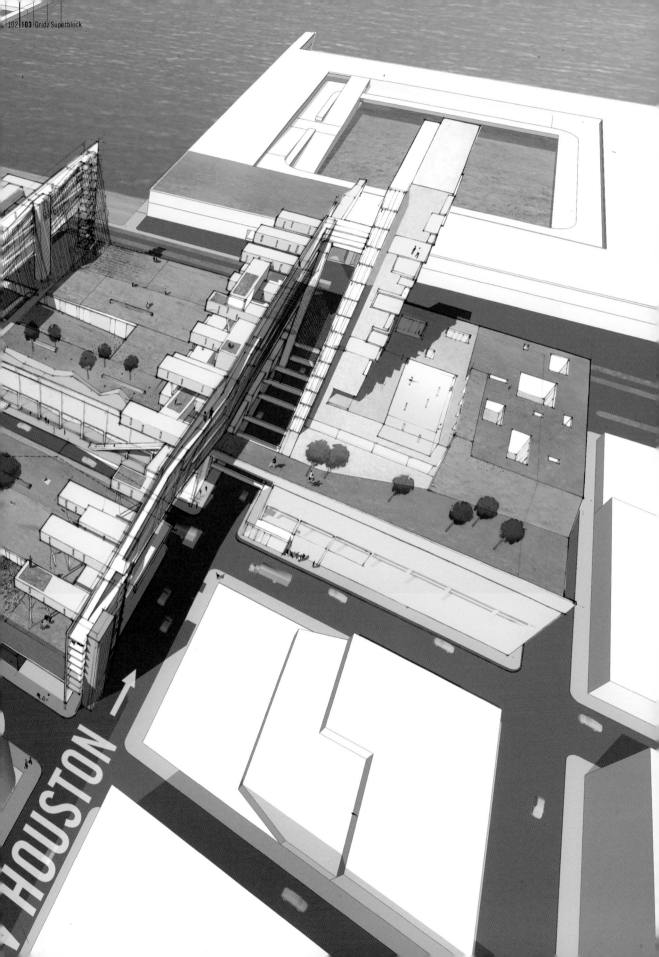

HOUSTON

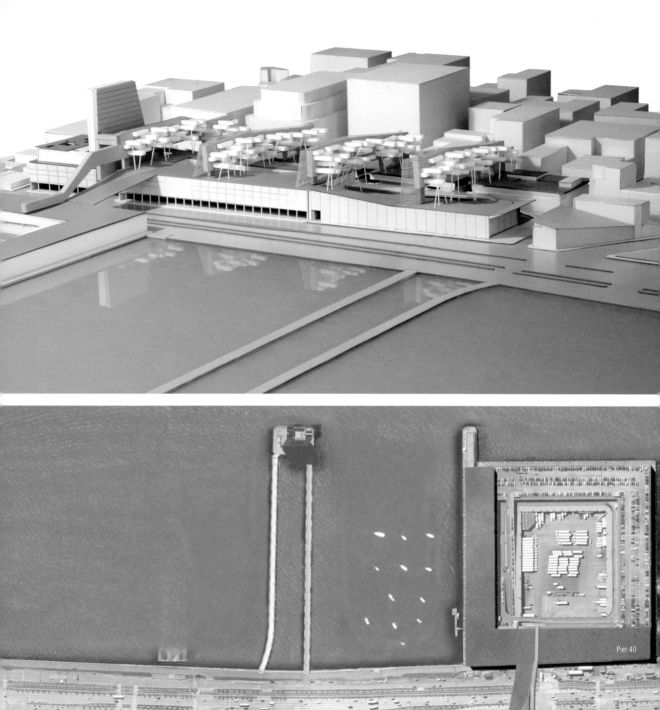

**Plan at superblock roofscape (+72')**

Pier 40

Land bridge to Pier 40

Housing bar above

Rooftop park

Hotel bar

Hotel pool

Cinema Café

Bridge to Pier

Office space

Office space

Office space

Spring St.

Vandam St.

Charlton St.

King St.

W. Houston St.

**Plan at elevated Washington Street (+28')**

New DSNY parking garage

Green roof

Pedestrian ramp

Office space

Office space

Retail space

Retail space

Retail space

Hotel bar

Hotel

Retail space

Retail space

Parking on UPS roof

Spring St.

Vandam St.

Charlton St.

King St.

W. Houston St.

N

**Plan at street level (+4')**

West St.

New DSNY parking garage

UPS facility

Office space

UPS facility

UPS office

Retail space

Hotel lobby

Spring St.

Vandam St.

Charlton St.

King St.

W. Houston St.

Sloped extensions of the existing historic street grid connect the old neighborhood to the elevated shopping street and raised green space. The existing UPS distribution facility continues to function at ground level, providing a vital service to the economy of the city.

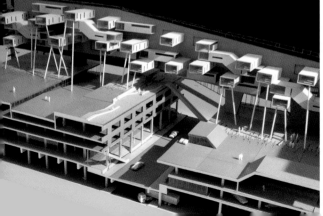

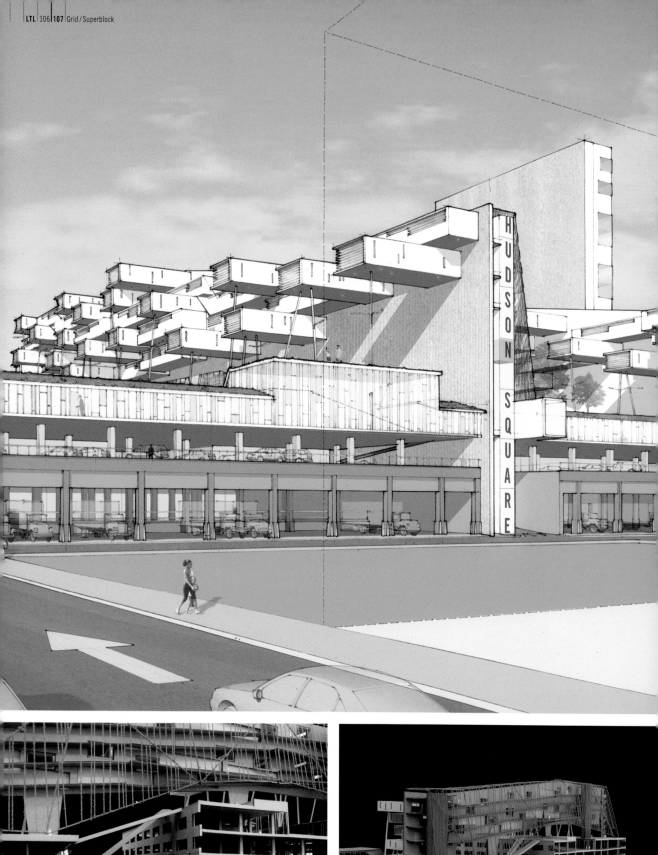

HUDSON SQUARE

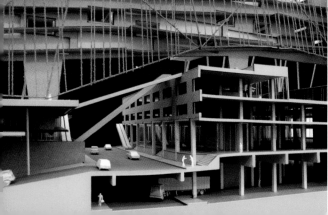

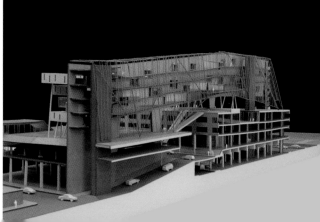

The cross section reveals the multilayered vertical urbanism generated by the superimposition of grid and superblock. Above, a series of housing units are arrayed to optimize southern exposures and riverfront views; they are linked by an elevated sidewalk that extends the east-west grid over the roofs of the superblocks. Below, the former rooftops function as a new public lawn and a series of community gardens. Voids within this elevated landscape allow for the penetration of daylight into the deep floor plates of the historic facilities, enabling more efficient utilization and improved environmental quality.

# Green Sponge

New York, New York

This project for a pragmatic yet utopian vision of district-wide sustainability was commissioned by Architecture Research Office as part of the Downtown Alliance's larger planning initiative for the Greenwich South neighborhood of Lower Manhattan. Based on an analysis of the flows of energy, water, air, food, excrement, and vegetation in the area, the project took two interrelated forms. The first was a narrative developed with the environmental engineer David White that identified the current state, near future, and ideal future of the district, establishing specific metrics and strategies for improving the environmental quality of Greenwich South, such as increased water conservation, building energy retrofits, reduction of automobile traffic, increased pedestrian and bicycle activity, and wetland induction. The second form was a series of design projects that articulated the potential sustainable future. These projects included the repurposing of a parking garage into an ecological center, complete with anaerobic processing of organic waste and a rooftop wetland; a bicycle epicenter that connects to the existing West Side bike path; and the Green Sponge, conceived as an atmospheric filter above the mouth of the Brooklyn Battery Tunnel. The Green Sponge is 150 feet by 150 feet by 400 feet and made from lightweight off-the-shelf scaffolding. The porous grid of scaffolding supports a heterogeneous array of plant species, birds, water-collection devices, and wind turbines, all interlaced with a series of light pedestrian walkways. Part park, part infrastructure, and part urban sculpture, the Green Sponge fills the void above the tunnel entrance with an inhabitable matrix of vegetation to mitigate the polluting effects of the traffic below.

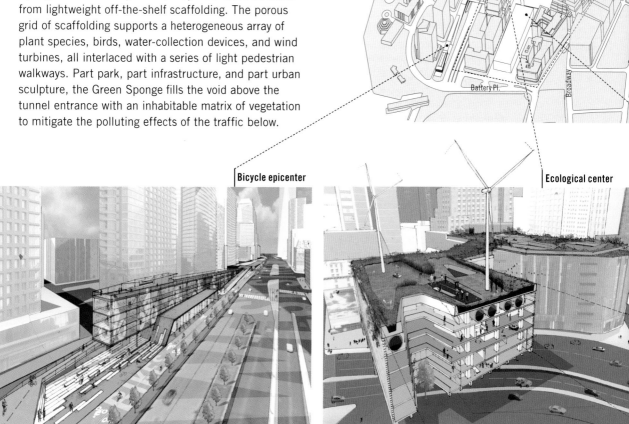

Bicycle epicenter

Ecological center

Green Sponge

# Glenmore Gardens

New York, New York

This collaborative project in East New York was a direct response to the challenge of providing well-designed, affordable, socially sustainable housing to an underserved neighborhood. Participating in the New Foundations program run by New York City's Department of Housing Preservation and Development, LTL worked in concert with three other firms—Architecture Research Office, BriggsKnowles Architecture + Design, and Della Valle Bernheimer (the developer and architect of record)—to transform five vacant lots into a vibrant community of ten low-cost homes. Together the four firms determined two distinct plan frameworks for the same duplex building type. From a consistent palette of inexpensive yet visually expressive materials, each firm created a unique approach to the public face of their respective duplex, balancing individuality and difference through the articulation of program and massing. Constructed for less than $105 per square foot, the Glenmore Gardens project demonstrates the capacity of architectural engagement to address low-cost housing with specificity and diversity.

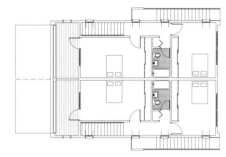

**Third-floor plan**

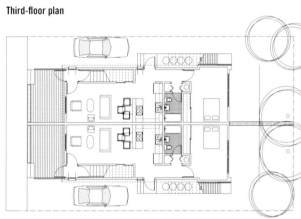

**First-floor plan**

Lewis.Tsurumaki.Lewis          Della Valle Bernheimer          BriggsKnowles Architecture + Design

**Owner-occupied unit**

**Rental unit**

Each duplex consists of a two-story, owner-occupied house above a rental unit. This creative programming reinforces the financial stability of the homeowner. LTL approached its duplex by identifying the owner's unit on the second and third floors through a distinct frame on the street facade, while cladding the rental unit below with cedar to provide warmth and tactility.

# Exhibit on Hollywood Boulevard

L.A. Forum for Architecture and Urban Design, Los Angeles, California

This exhibition was located in a storefront on Hollywood Boulevard. In order to mimic the glorification of plan enacted by the embedded stars of the Walk of Fame, the installation carved the plans of four LTL projects into a new floor that ran down the center of the gallery. The projects, which varied in scale from 69 million square feet to 108 square feet, were positioned from largest to smallest, starting at the street. The floor's width also decreased as one moved into the gallery. Anchored to the floor and stretched to the wall, images related to each project were backlit by a field of fluorescent lights. This forced perspective, with illuminated gill-like spaces, made the exhibit appear longer when viewed from Hollywood Boulevard.

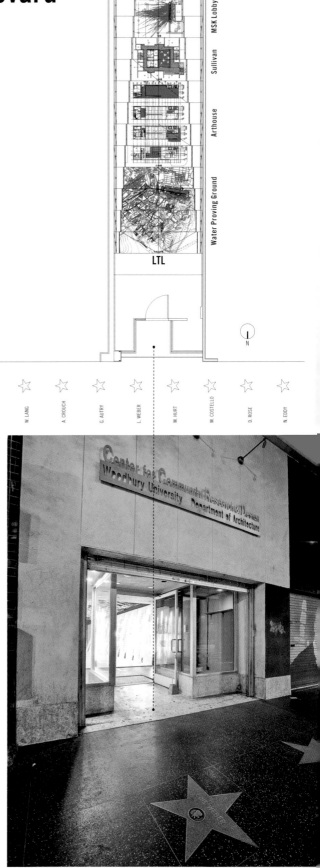

# Department of Social and Cultural Analysis

New York, New York

New York University's Department of Social and Cultural Analysis (SCA) is interdisciplinary in nature, addressing topics and methodologies drawn from the humanities and social sciences. Its concentrations include Africana Studies, Asian/Pacific/American Studies, Gender and Sexuality Studies, and Metropolitan Studies. This project involved the design of a new 16,400-square-foot headquarters that would gather this diverse faculty in a single space for the first time. The variety of departmental identities made it vital that the design optimize the possibilities for interaction and collaboration within an existing floor plate, enabling faculty from different disciplines to engage with students and one another in a range of settings.

 The brief—which included faculty and administrative offices, meeting rooms, and student spaces—called for maximizing the available square footage, locating faculty offices at the perimeter of the plan to allow access to windows. Although this is a conventional approach to office design, it typically results in corridors deprived of daylight and visual interest, and the deep floor plate that was to serve as the SCA site would exacerbate this tendency. The design therefore proposed to carve away these perimeter offices at strategic locations to introduce natural light to the interior of the plan and produce a series of public rooms. These collective spaces would enliven and expand the hallways and facilitate social interaction at multiple scales—from larger common areas to more intimate spaces for discussion and collaboration. The design thus operates on a principle of removal rather than addition, beginning with the most efficient programmatic distribution and then selectively eroding the plan to generate open space.

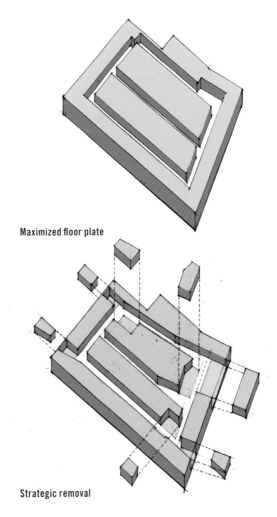

**Maximized floor plate**

**Strategic removal**

**Floor plan**

N

In order to capitalize on the unique qualities of the given site, the enclosed rooms were treated as volumes inserted below the existing steel and concrete barrel vaults, which remained exposed in the circulation zones. This architectural feature—revealed during demolition—provides a sense of continuity throughout the public areas while maximizing ceiling heights. Below this unifying surface, two main volumes house graduate student offices, meeting rooms, and classrooms. The ends of the larger volume were excavated to produce separate lounge areas for faculty and students and a new reception desk, all defined by continuous bamboo surfaces. While the bamboo ceiling is perforated for ambient lighting, the floor surface slopes upward to form a sculptural seating element.

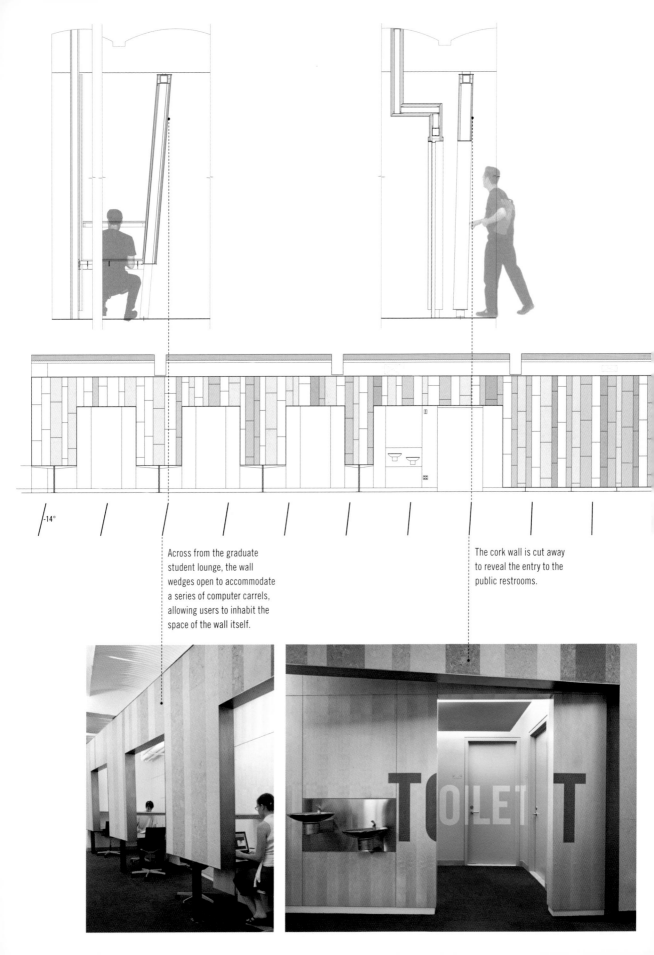

-14°

Across from the graduate
student lounge, the wall
wedges open to accommodate
a series of computer carrels,
allowing users to inhabit the
space of the wall itself.

The cork wall is cut away
to reveal the entry to the
public restrooms.

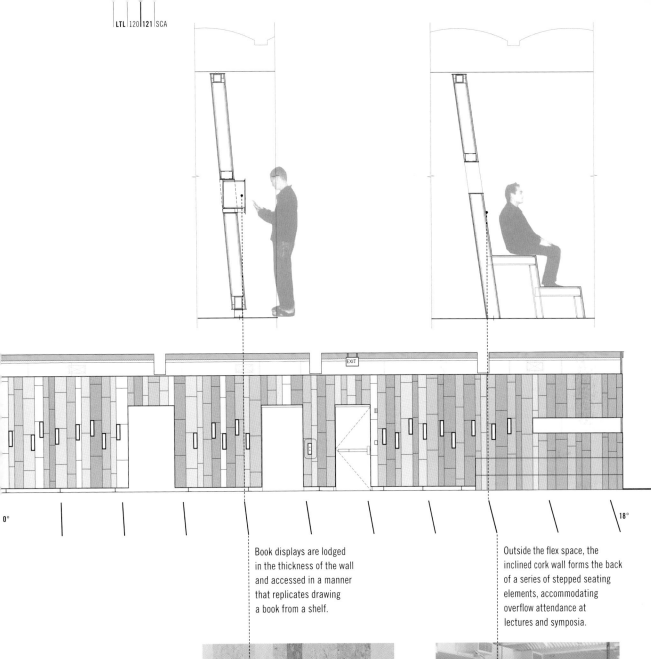

0°                                                                                          18°

Book displays are lodged
in the thickness of the wall
and accessed in a manner
that replicates drawing
a book from a shelf.

Outside the flex space, the
inclined cork wall forms the back
of a series of stepped seating
elements, accommodating
overflow attendance at
lectures and symposia.

Adjoining the entry and reception is a torquing
wall clad in cork strips of varied color and
width. A continuous ruled surface, the wall
is vertical only at its midpoint, leaning in
opposite directions at its extreme ends. At
its eastern end, adjacent to a large multiuse
flex space, the cork wall is calibrated to the
angle of a seat back, creating stepped seating
for events, and wraps down to produce the
floor surface. As it twists along the length
of the major public hall, it splits and folds to
house bathrooms, copy rooms, and computer
workstations. The cork wall provides a sense
of continuity and identity while transforming
locally to accommodate a diversity of needs.

In the corner with the best light and views, the large flex space serves alternately as a lecture hall and a lounge for students and faculty. A series of sliding resin panels allows for varying degrees of enclosure without sacrificing the transmission of daylight. In its daily use as an informal commons, it is open to the adjacent circulation and reception areas; however it can also be closed off from the adjoining corridor during lectures and events.

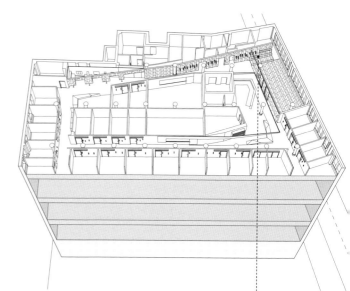

The hallways are wide enough to facilitate both circulation and casual interaction; their breadth also mitigates their length. Natural light enters the otherwise internalized spaces through clerestories and a series of translucent bookcases inserted through the walls shared by the faculty offices and the corridors. These colored acrylic boxes provide supplemental bookshelves inside the offices and room identification in the hallway. The translucent material makes the books visible from the public hall, permitting passing students to view selected titles from their professors' collections.

# Claremont University Consortium
## Administrative Campus Center

Claremont, California

This new Administrative Campus Center for the Claremont University Consortium (CUC) consolidates the majority of CUC departments and services, previously dispersed and fragmented across the campus, into a single location. The adaptive reuse of an underutilized 42,000-square-foot maintenance building provides CUC with an environmentally sensitive and vibrant work area that has a well-defined public character and creates a collective gathering place for the colleges and the broader community.

The project deploys a series of intertwined, materially rich, tactical elements that transform the existing facility and redefine its public presence. These include a 740-foot-long cedar screen, a custom ceiling cloud, a digital garden, and a field of 168 solar chimneys that provide natural light throughout the space. While a major aspect of the project's sustainability strategy is retaining and reusing the existing prefabricated steel shed, its current utilitarian exterior is neither inviting nor appropriate for the new use. To redefine the building's character, a continuous cedar surface wraps portions of its north, east, and south elevations. The ribbon works with the original pitch-roofed geometry of the building, but slips free of its shell to produce a clearly defined entry point along with a series of outdoor gathering spaces. Moving from exterior to interior, the cedar screen defines the major public circulation and shared facilities. Illuminated at night with embedded LED lights, the cedar ribbon serves as both a wayfinding device—denoting the building's entry to vehicular and pedestrian traffic—and as a recognizable image for CUC.

**Existing building**

Defining both exterior and interior spaces, the cedar ribbon exists in dialog with the existing building envelope. On the north, the screen is folded to create a shaded patio that takes advantage of the Southern California climate. At the entrance, the ribbon slips into the interior, framing a new reception area and café, then continues out to the south patio, where it defines a large multipurpose area protected from the weather by a tensile structure covered with translucent fabric. When passing over windows, the spacing of the cedar panels is increased to allow light in.

**East elevation**

**Floor plan**

The interior exploits both the high ceiling and the large spans of the existing steel structure, providing an open office space with custom furniture for more than one hundred employees. Containing a range of different-size meeting rooms, the building also functions as a shared conference facility for Claremont Colleges. Taking advantage of an existing mechanical mezzanine that broke up the continuity of the interior, the bulk of these conference rooms was consolidated into one central volume inflected by the space's primary circulation routes and surfaced in an interactive LED art installation.

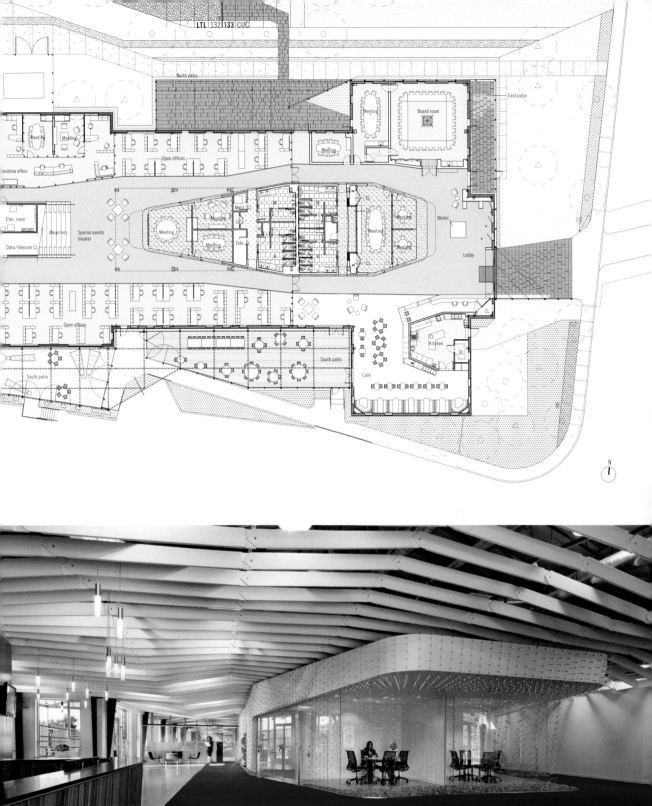

North patio

LTL 132 133 CUC

East patio

Meeting

Board room

Meeting

Meeting

Meeting

Open offices

Executive office

Meeting

Meeting

Model

Meeting

Meeting

Elec. room

Meeting

Bleachers

Special events theater

Meeting

Meeting

Lobby

Data / telecom CL

Ele. CL

CL

Open offices

CL

South patio

Kitchen

St.

South patio

Café

N

A wide stair emerges from a central spine of red carpet, providing
bleacher-like seating for large gatherings. Hidden underneath
the stairs is an existing electrical room, while vertical electrical
conduits and a cactus garden inhabit the space above the stairs.

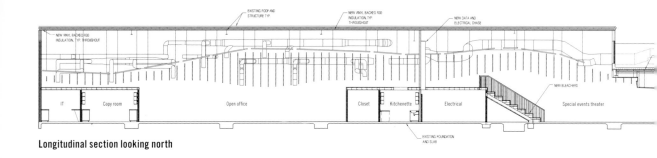

Longitudinal section looking north

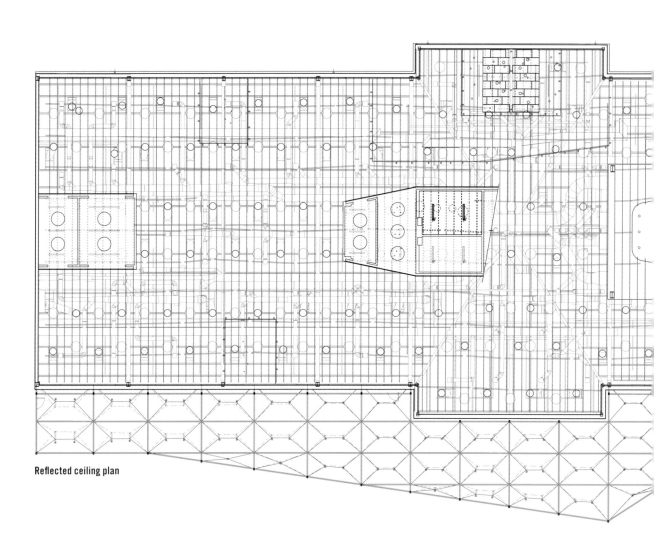

Reflected ceiling plan

In contrast to the open quality of
the floor plan, the reflected ceiling plan
is intricate and complex. Whereas
the floor is a thin surface, the ceiling is of
multilayered thickness, distributing air,
light, electricity, and data while producing
optical, acoustic, and geometric effects.

NEW & EXISTING MECH
EQPT, SEE MECH DWGS

NEW & EXISTING MECH
EQPT, SEE MECH DWGS

MECHANICAL EQPT ABOVE
HUNG CEILING, SEE MECH
DWGS

MECHANICAL EQPT ABOVE
SEE MECH DWGS

NEW VINYL BACKED
R30 INSULATION

MECHANICAL EQPT ABOVE
ACOUSTICAL BAFFLES, SEE
MECH DWGS

SEE MECH DWGS FOR NEW
CURB LOCATION AND DETAILS

EXISTING CURB
LOCATION

EXISTING ROOF AND
STRUCTURE TYP.

EXISTING
MECHANICAL
MEZZANINE

EXISTING
STRUCTURE

HUNG DWB CEILING

NEW CEDAR
CLADDING

EXISTING
CONCRETE DECK

EXISTING R-30
INSULATION TO REMAIN

SUSPENDED
ACOUSTICAL BAFFLE

DWB-03      DWB-03      DWB-03      DWB-03

| Meeting room | Closet | Men's WC | Men's WC | CL | Meeting room | Meeting room | Lobby | Entry |

EXISTING FOUNDATION
AND SLAB

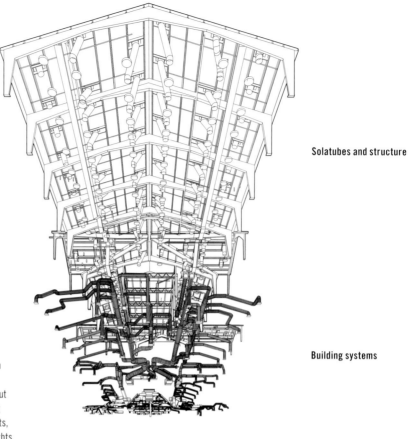

Solatubes and structure

Building systems

Using 168 Solatube skylights in combination with
expanded windows along the perimeter, there is
enough natural light to work at all stations without
artificial lighting during the day, greatly reducing
the building's energy consumption. As the sun sets,
a grid of high-efficiency dimmable fluorescent lights
slowly turns on, maintaining a consistent level of
illumination. To allow the light to filter into the space,
a custom ceiling is composed of nearly 1,500 9-foot-
long by 8-inch-high baffles, which are clad in felt
made from recycled plastic bottles. The ceiling unifies
the space, forming a sculpted interior cloud across
the entire building that obscures the infrastructure
and assists with sound mitigation in the open office.

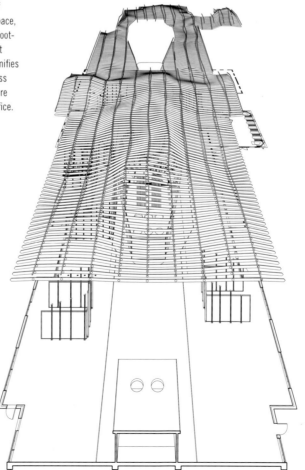

Ceiling cloud

Floor objects

Existing space

Building systems and Solatubes

Ceiling cloud of baffles

7:00 a.m.

9:00 a.m.

11:00 a.m.

1:00 p.m.

3:00 p.m.

5:00 p.m.

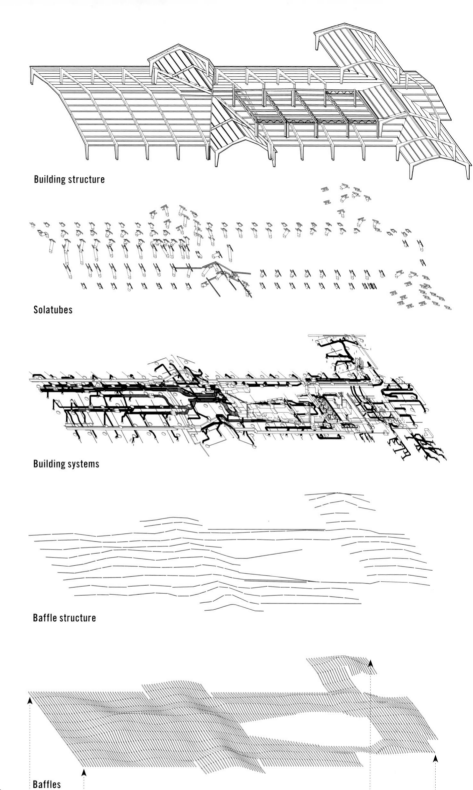

**Building structure**

**Solatubes**

**Building systems**

**Baffle structure**

**Baffles**

This project is an architecture made almost entirely of materialized lines. Cumulatively, ceiling baffles, cedar slats, and cables strung with LED lights aggregate into continuous surfaces and volumes, but upon closer inspection, these conditions dissolve and the elements reappear individually as their constituent parts.

**Partitions and floor elements**

A digital garden installation, produced by
the artist Jason Krugman and comprised
of more than six thousand LED modules,
envelops the central core of meeting
rooms. The LEDs are triggered by the
motion of people walking nearby, and
subtly shift from green to blue and
back to green. As one moves around the
installation the perception of the LEDs as
an assemblage also shifts from a crisp
line to a surface to a porous thickness.

# The Buffet
## at the MGM CityCenter

Las Vegas, Nevada

LTL was one of a number of architects and designers selected to participate in the creation of one of the largest private developments in America: the MGM CityCenter in Las Vegas. The collective design teams' charge was to conceive a new urban entity for Las Vegas, where carefully considered contemporary design could provide an alternative to the shallow theme-park concepts that have dominated the Strip. LTL's assigned challenge was to rethink the typical Las Vegas buffet by enhancing the dining experience and facilitating social interaction while maintaining the performance standards of the 600-seat all-you-can-eat venue. At the heart of the problem was a tension between the need to break the 23,600-square-foot dining floor into smaller, more intimate seating areas and the desire to preserve a clear line of sight across the entire space, leading all customers to the food stations and providing a view to the pool landscape beyond. While the plan, organized by a series of built-in banquettes, determined efficiencies of program and designated seating areas, the primary design was executed in section. A sculpted, white, cloudlike ceiling drops down to align with the high points of the banquettes, creating a sense of a private dining room for those who are seated while framing a clear view corridor through the buffet for customers moving through the space.

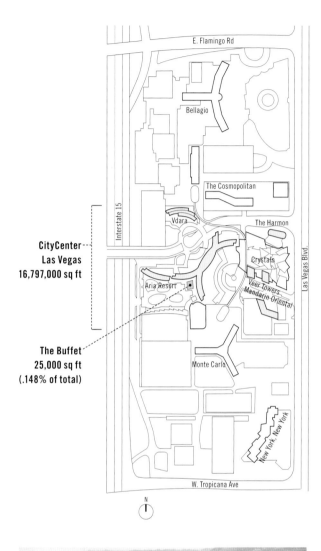

CityCenter
Las Vegas
16,797,000 sq ft

The Buffet
25,000 sq ft
(.148% of total)

**Food troughs**
**+**
**Horizontal eat zone**

**Aria Resort**

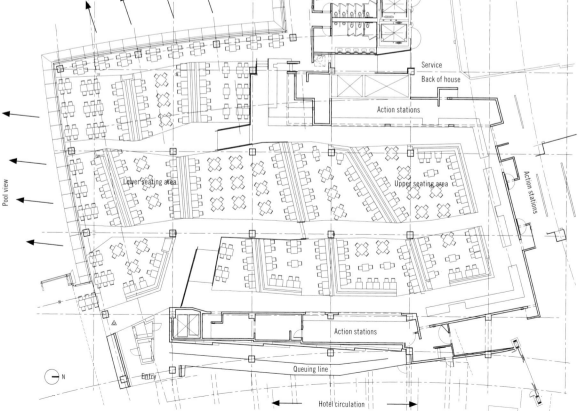

Pool view

Service

Back of house

Action stations

Lower seating area

Upper seating area

Action stations

Pool view

Action stations

Entry

Queuing line

Hotel circulation

N

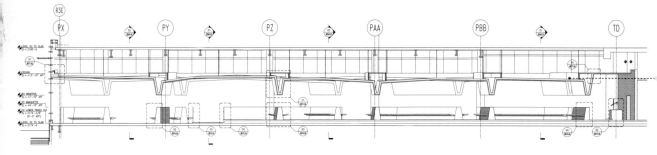

**Section looking west**

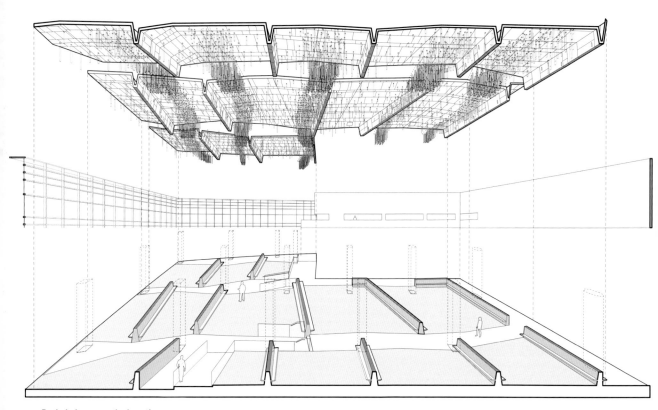

**Exploded perspectival section**

Changes in section drive the design for the buffet.
A sculpted ground organized through bamboo
banquettes extends up from the floor plane,
matched by an undulating series of illuminated
ceiling ribbons. Together they define the primary
spatial and functional areas of the buffet yet
never physically touch, leaving a consistent
open slot across the dining area that aligns with
the openings of the food service stations.

## Reflected ceiling plan

The ceiling is the primary articulated surface in the buffet that
reinforces designated functional areas. The main ribbons of the
ceiling, made of backlit acoustical panels covered in Xorel fabric,
are broken to align with the paths between the dining areas
and the service station. Circular lights cut across the ribbons in
clusters of edge-lit Pyrex tubes in the gaps above the circulation
aisles, animating and illuminating the large buffet space.

**Dessert**

**Main**

| Salad

Entry |

A single, continuous wall, wrapped in an interlocking pattern of glass tiles, forms the surface of exchange between diners and chefs. The wall shifts in color balance from green to orange, linking the queuing line at the entry with the dessert station at the far end. Sculptural deformations of the wall at the entry queue reveal video displays to the patrons waiting in line.

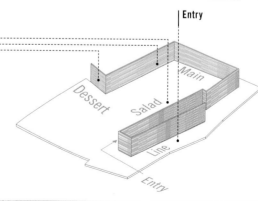

# Birdhouse

Plano, Illinois

Mies van der Rohe's Farnsworth House (1951), while a model of transparency, has had unintended and deadly consequences for the local avian population, which, to its detriment, seems unaware of the structure's importance. This design shifts the function of the glass walls to sponsor the inhabitation of nature in the form of living birds. The ornamentation of the house is derived from commonplace bird-saver stickers, typically applied to large expanses of glass to help prevent accidental collisions. Here, the surface applications are extruded from the glass walls as a series of projections, which enshroud the pure form of the house in functional spines. These elements have multiple uses: They produce a visual opacity that varies according to the observer's position on the site and the degree of privacy of the enclosed program. They act as a pixelated solar shading for the glass walls and serve as birdbaths, feeders, and even birdhouses, collecting rainwater for drinking and providing locations for nesting. The notoriously inhospitable house acquires a layer of inhabited ornamentation that attracts and supports the fauna of the site.

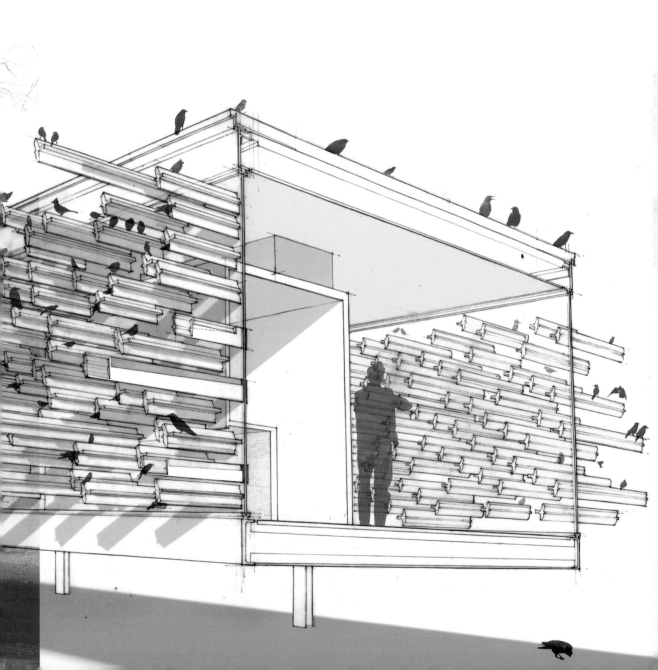

# Arthouse
## at the Jones Center

Austin, Texas

Renovations of century-old buildings of architectural merit often attempt to reconstitute particular moments of history. For this contemporary art space, however, LTL embraced the trajectory of the existing construction's transformation, rather than returning it to a moment frozen in time. Located in the heart of downtown Austin, Arthouse is a renovation of a 1920s theater that was later modified into a department store in the 1950s. During the midcentury conversion, the building's open structure, consisting of a concrete frame with steel trusses, was altered to include a single-story, steel-supported concrete deck. This second-floor addition cut in half the theater's large proscenium space. Adding 14,000 square feet of new program to the existing art space, LTL intensified this accumulation of history by conceiving of the design as a series of further tactical additions and adjustments. These supplements revive and augment extant features—such as the trusses, concrete frame, and ornamental interior frescoes from the 1920s, as well as the awning, storefront, and upper-level display window from the 1950s.

Concrete frame with steel trusses

**Queen Theater, 1926**

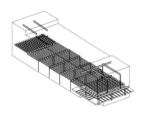

Steel frame with concrete floor

**Lerner Shops, 1956**

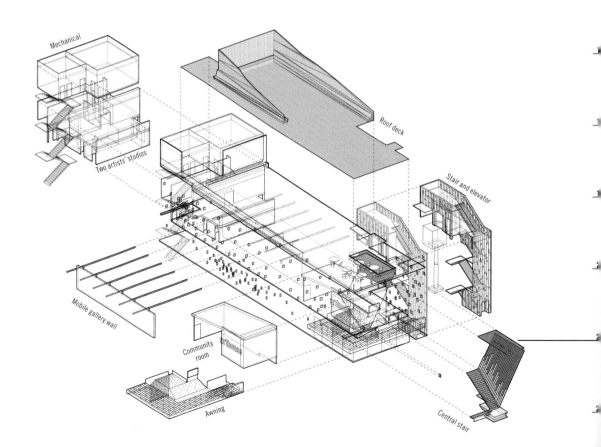

Mechanical

Two artists' studios

Roof deck

Stair and elevator

Mobile gallery wall

Community room

Awning

Central stair

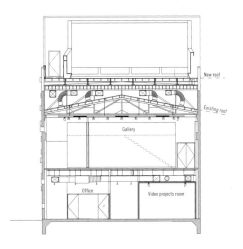

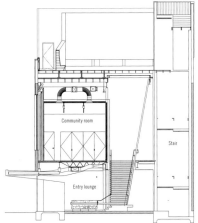

**Cross sections looking west**

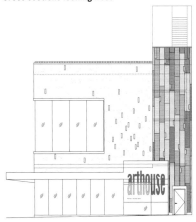

**West elevation**

The building's envelope intensifies exchanges between the city and Arthouse. The entry lounge is wrapped in glass, maximizing sidewalk exposure and allowing glimpses into both floors of galleries. The 1950s awning is functionally enhanced not only by creating shade and capturing sidewalk territory outside, but also by extending into the building. Here, vertical tabs added at the entry provide the surface for the sheared sign, inviting visitors to enter Arthouse through its name. The large opening of the second floor community room doubles as a projection screen visible from the street at night.

arthouse
arthouse
Arthouse at the Jones Center
cozzoli's pizza

The majority of the existing building's elevations lacked windows, as a theater and a department store do not require natural light. Similarly, gallery spaces demand few windows. Therefore, a new form of aperture, based on accumulation and density, was developed to unify the building and create a logical yet unconventional facade appropriate for an experimental art venue. The southern and eastern elevations are perforated by 177 glass blocks, which are lodged in the existing masonry. The density of perforations is increased where more light is needed—offices, studios, meeting rooms—and decreased where light is less desired, as in the galleries and lecture room. Set within the infill of the concrete frame, the density and locations of the blocks telegraph the structure and program of the building through its skin. During the day, luminous shadows cast by the cantilevered blocks animate the exterior stucco surface, while at night individually programmable LED lights illuminate the blocks from within the wall thickness. Inside, the blocks augment the existing theater frescoes and remaining traces of the department store, adding a new bespoke layer to the accumulated surface.

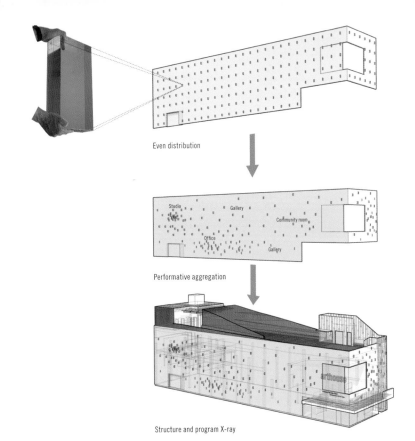

Even distribution

Performative aggregation

Structure and program X-ray

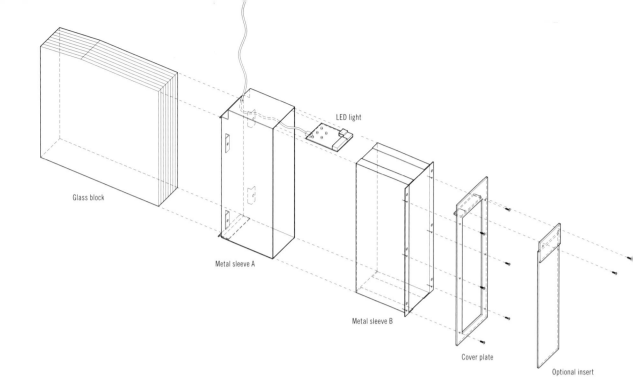

Glass block

LED light

Metal sleeve A

Metal sleeve B

Cover plate

Optional insert

**LED lights:** Each block is illuminated by two green and three white LED lights, which are fed power and data through a dedicated cat-5 cable and are capable of being individually programmed, varying intensity and pattern across the building's elevations.

**Glass blocks:** The blocks were made by laminating ½ inch-thick glass. All 177 blocks are 4 inches wide and 16 inches high, but vary from 11 ¾ inches to 46 ¾ inches deep, based on the wall's thickness and the amount of cantilever beyond the building. As layers of glass, the blocks transmit and refract sunlight into arcs on the floor.

**Holes:** Due to the concrete frame of the existing building, holes for the glass blocks were cut out of the infill masonry wall with a chain saw. Each block was then sealed into an interlocked telescoping steel sleeve, whose two halves were inserted into the hole from the inside and outside of the wall.

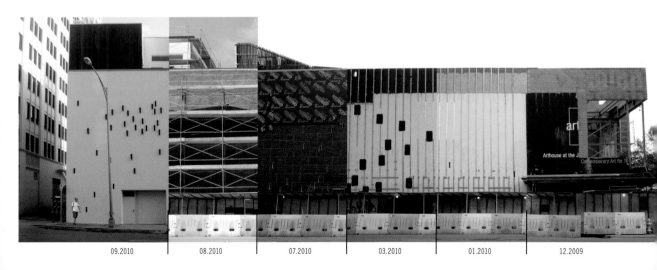
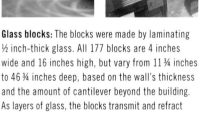

| 09.2010 | 08.2010 | 07.2010 | 03.2010 | 01.2010 | 12.2009 |

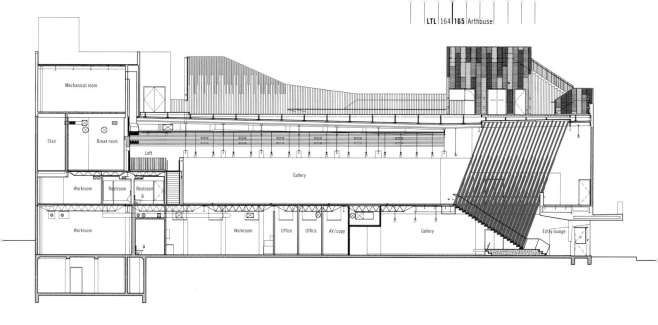

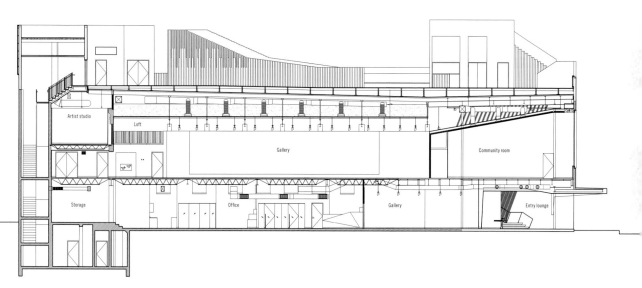

**Longitudinal sections looking north**

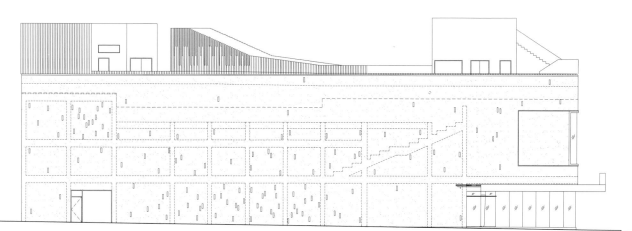

**North elevation**

The central stair provides the primary spatial connection between the entry lobby and the second-floor gallery. Its lower three treads are cast-in-place concrete while the upper twenty-one ipe wood treads are suspended from above, connected visually and physically to a skylight in the roof deck. The lowermost wood tread is elongated into the reception desk, while the concrete base is extended to offer an area for sitting. The staircase is both playful and grand, floating and grounded, expansive and local.

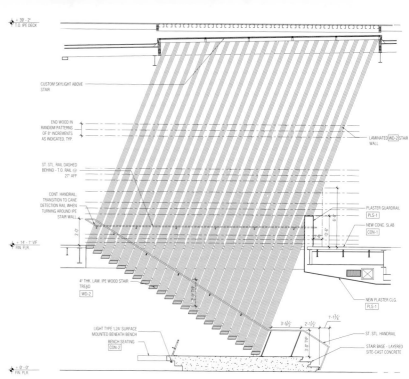

**Stair section**

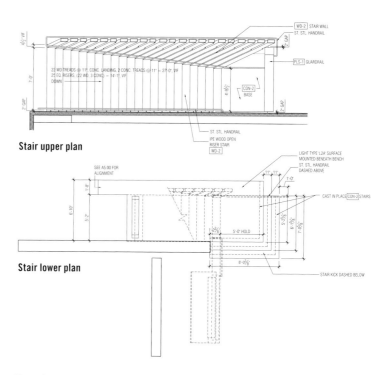

**Stair upper plan**

**Stair lower plan**

Ranging in length from twenty-five to thirty-eight feet, the stair treads were fabricated off site and individually mounted in the floor cavity. Given its size and complexity, the staircase was installed prior to the construction of walls on the upper floor. The horizontal treads are composed of glue-laminated ipe wood strips, each forming a rhombus in section in order to dovetail into the inclined vertical. This joint is reinforced by embedding steel within the laminations.

The stair is inclined in two axes, toward the north and east. The angle of the slope is derived from the geometry of the stair nosing, thereby using the logic of a minor detail to inform the overall form. At any horizontal cut, the volume of the staircase is a rectangle. Yet, due to the inclined verticals, the stair is five feet wide at the lowest tread and seven feet wide at the top. The stair expands as one ascends from the street level to the main second-floor gallery, where the street remains visible from the top of the staircase.

10.2010

In the main gallery, a thirteen-foot-high by fifty-five-foot-long wall is suspended from I-beams that were required to stiffen the bottom chords of the existing steel trusses. Using motorized trollies, the gallery can be quickly reconfigured from a single space that reveals the textured southern wall to a more conventional white-walled gallery. Alternatively, the wall can be used to split the gallery into two, or to form a constricted tunnel-like space adjacent to one of the exterior walls.

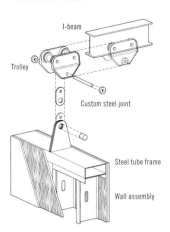

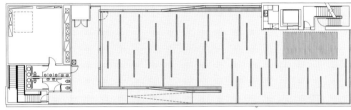

**Roof-deck plan**

04.2011

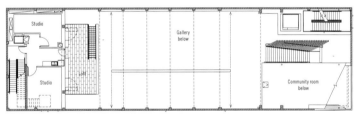

**Mezzanine plan**

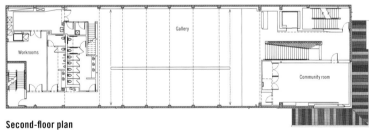

**Second-floor plan**

11.2011

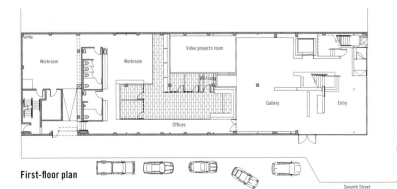

**First-floor plan**

The roof deck is constructed as a large, integrated piece of millwork with benches that morph into a vertical enclosure, defining a space for gathering. The deck can host a range of events, from outdoor film screenings and music performances to informal dinners and formal weddings, all outside yet embedded within the heart of downtown Austin.

The custom furniture for the two reception desks and a lectern incorporates the pattern of the exterior elevation on stainless steel modesty panels, while the angle of the legs matches the slope of the central staircase.

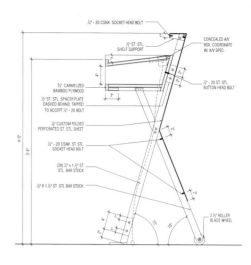

½" - 20 CSNK. SOCKET HEAD BOLT

CONCEALED A/V BOX, COORDINATE W/ A/V SPEC.

½" ST. STL. SHELF SUPPORT

½" - 20 ST. STL. BUTTON HEAD BOLT

¾" CARMELIZED BAMBOO PLYWOOD

½" ST. STL. SPACER PLATE DASHED BEHIND, TAPPED TO ACCEPT ½" - 20 BOLT

⅛" CUSTOM FOLDED PERFORATED ST. STL. SHEET

½" - 20 CSNK. ST. STL. SOCKET HEAD BOLT

(2X) ½" x 1 ½" ST. STL. BAR STOCK

½" X 1 ½" ST. STL. BAR STOCK

2 ½" ROLLER BLADE WHEEL

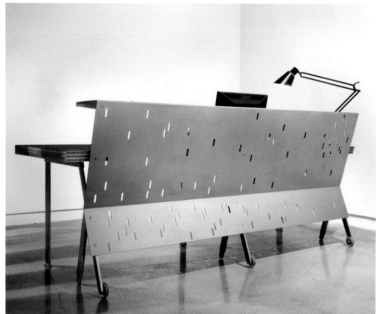

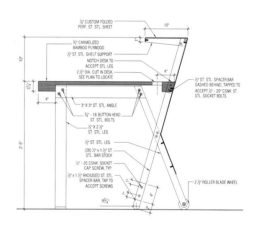

⅛" CUSTOM FOLDED PERF. ST. STL. SHEET

10"

¾" CARMELIZED BAMBOO PLYWOOD

½" ST. STL. SHELF SUPPORT

NOTCH DESK TO ACCEPT STL. LEG

2 ½" DIA. CUT IN DESK, SEE PLAN TO LOCATE

½" ST. STL. SPACER BAR DASHED BEHIND, TAPPED TO ACCEPT ½" - 20" CSNK. ST. STL. SOCKET BOLTS

3" X 3" ST. STL. ANGLE

⅜" - 16 BUTTON HEAD ST. STL. BOLTS

½" X 2 ½" ST. STL. LEG

½" ST. STL. LEG

(2X) ½" x 1 ½" ST. STL. BAR STOCK

½" - 20 CSNK. SOCKET CAP SCREW, TYP.

½" x 1 ½" RADIUSED ST. STL. SPACER BAR, TAP TO ACCEPT SCREWS

2 ½" ROLLER BLADE WHEEL

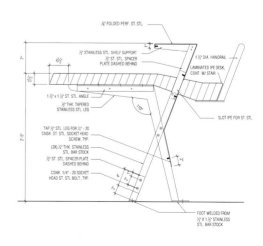

⅛" FOLDED PERF. ST. STL.

½" STAINLESS STL. SHELF SUPPORT

½" ST. STL. SPACER PLATE DASHED BEHIND

1 ½" DIA. HANDRAIL

LAMINATED IPE DESK, CONT. W/ STAIR

1 ½" x 1 ½" ST. STL. ANGLE

½" THK. TAPERED STAINLESS STL. LEG

SLOT IPE FOR ST. STL.

TAP ½" STL. LEG FOR ½" - 20 CNSK. ST. STL. SOCKET HEAD SCREW, TYP.

(2X) ½" THK. STAINLESS STL. BAR STOCK

½" ST. STL. SPACER PLATE DASHED BEHIND

CSNK. 1/4" - 20 SOCKET HEAD ST. STL. BOLT, TYP.

FOOT WELDED FROM ½" X 1 ½" STAINLESS STL. BAR STOCK

Designed and fabricated by LTL, twenty-one
pieces of mobile lounge furniture can be variously
configured, from a single seat to landscape-like
assemblies. The interlocking shapes are raked in
two directions consistent with the central staircase
and are surfaced in layers of industrial felt.

**Elevator:** As a sectional device within the building, the elevator reveals the vertical extension of the central staircase and the alignment between the stair and the pattern of the skylight in the roof deck.

**Community room:** The community room has the capacity to accommodate a range of programs, from meetings to lectures to art classes. The rectangular volume extrudes from the glass wall facing Congress Avenue into the building. Blackout rear and front projection screens can be extracted from pockets in the wall, allowing animation of both the building's interior and exterior.

**Use:** The entire building is designed for maximum programmatic
flexibility. Moreover, the building accommodates a range
of densities of use, from a single visitor engaged with the
art to crowds watching films on the rooftop, gathering for
an event in the second-floor gallery, or dancing in the entry
lobby (enticing the curiosity of sidewalk passersby).

# Project Credits

2007–12

**Canopy Connection**, 2011–, Laramie, WY
Client: College of Education, University of Wyoming
Project team: Paul Lewis, Marc Tsurumaki, David J. Lewis; John Morrison, project
  manager; Kristen Chin, Diana Mera Hernando, Kenneth Wong, Carrie Schulz
Architect of record: University of Wyoming Facilities Planning Office
Structural engineer: Robert Silman Associates
MEP: MKK Consulting Engineers
Glazing consultant: Front, Inc.

**Carnegie Library Public Spaces**, 2011–, Syracuse, NY
Client: Syracuse University
Project team: Paul Lewis, Marc Tsurumaki, David J. Lewis; Emily Greene, project
  manager; John Loercher, Jason Dannenbring, Perla Dís Kristinsdóttir,
  Deric Mizokami, Hye-Young Chung, Matthew Clarke, Tarlton Long
Mechanical engineer: Peterson Guadagnolo Consulting Engineers
Lighting design: LumenArch
Structural engineer: Klepper, Hahn & Hyatt

**Department of Architecture Offices**, 2011–, Ithaca, NY
Client: Cornell University
Project team: Paul Lewis, Marc Tsurumaki, David J. Lewis; Kristen Chin, Kevin Hayes,
  David Temidara
Mechanical engineer: LaBella Associates
Contractor: Welliver

**Gallaudet University Living and Learning Residence Hall 6**, 2010–, Washington, DC
Client: Gallaudet University
Project team: Paul Lewis, Marc Tsurumaki, David J. Lewis; Clark Manning, project
  manager; Carrie Schulz, Jason Dannenbring, John Morrison, Elena Koroleva,
  Chelsea Livingston

Architect of record: Quinn Evans Architects
Design-build contractor: SIGAL Construction Corporation
Structural engineer: Robert Silman Associates
Mechanical engineer: Setty and Associates International
Civil engineer: Delon Hampton and Associates

**Dean House Pavilion**, 2010–, Miami Beach, FL
Client: William Dean
Project team: Paul Lewis, Marc Tsurumaki, David J. Lewis; Hye-Young Chung,
  Jason Dannenbring, Clark Manning, Carrie Schulz, Jeff White, Chelsea Livingston,
  Danielle Pecora
Executive architect: Dale Overmyer Architects
Structural engineer: Robert Silman Associates
Lighting designer: LumenArch

**Steinhardt School of Culture, Education, and Human Development Renovation**,
2010–, New York, NY
Client: New York University
Project team: Paul Lewis, Marc Tsurumaki, David J. Lewis; Clark Manning, project
  architect; Jason Dannenbring, Carrie Schulz, Kristen Alexander, Keith Greenwald,
  Kevin Hayes, Perla Dís Kristindóttir, Hye-Young Chung
Structural engineer: Robert Silman Associates
Mechanical engineer: Thomas Polise Consulting Engineer
Lighting designer: Tillotson Design Associates
Environmental designer: Design360
A/V consultant: The Sextant Group
LEED consultant: Steven Winter Associates
Construction manager: Structure Tone

## Gallaudet University Living and Learning Residence Hall 6

**NEF163 Fitness**, 2010–, Istanbul, Turkey
Client: Timur Gayrimenkul Yatırım A.S.
Project team: Paul Lewis, Marc Tsurumaki, David J. Lewis; Perla Dís Kristinsdóttir,
Kevin Hayes, Jason Dannenbring, Carrie Schulz, Kristen Chin

**Bird Library Classrooms**, 2009–, Syracuse, NY
Client: Syracuse University
Project team: Paul Lewis, Marc Tsurumaki, David J. Lewis; Perla Dís Kristinsdóttir,
project manager; Emily Greene, project manager; Jon Schramm, John Loercher,
Nick Safley
Mechanical engineer: Peterson Guadagnolo Consulting Engineers

**Memorial Sloan-Kettering Lobby Wall**, 2005–, New York, NY
Client: Memorial Sloan-Kettering
Project team: Paul Lewis, Marc Tsurumaki, David J. Lewis; Jason Dannenbring, project
manager; Alex Terzich, project manager; Matthew Roman
Art advisor: Nancy Rosen
Building architect: Skidmore, Owings and Merrill
Fabricator: Veyko

**LTL Architects–Recent Work**, February 22–March 9, 2012, Bristol, RI
Client: School of Architecture, Art and Historic Preservation, Roger Williams University
Project team: Paul Lewis, Marc Tsurumaki, David J. Lewis; Elizabeth Kuwada
Exhibit coordinator: Daniel Alexander

**LTL Architects–Recent Work**, February 8–24, 2012, Berkeley, CA
Client: College of Environmental Design, University of California, Berkeley
Project team: Paul Lewis, Marc Tsurumaki, David J. Lewis; Elizabeth Kuwada
Exhibit coordinator: Keith Plymale

**LTL Architects–Exhibition**, January 17–March 5, 2012, Wooster, OH
Client: College of Wooster Art Museum
Project team: Paul Lewis, Marc Tsurumaki, David J. Lewis; Elizabeth Kuwada,
Kristen Chin, Mercedes Cuvi
Curator: Kitty McManus Zurko

**Catholic University School of Architecture Competition**, 2011–12, Washington, DC
Client: Catholic University
Project team: Paul Lewis, Marc Tsurumaki, David J. Lewis; Emily Greene, Jessie Turnbull,
Irene Brisson, Naoki Kamitani, Ting Ting Jin, Alan Ford, Clare Reidy, Kristen Chin

**Downtown Houston Central Station Design Competition**, 2011–12, Houston, TX
Client: Metropolitan Transit Authority of Harris Country, Houston Rapid Transit and
Downtown Management District
Project team: Paul Lewis, Marc Tsurumaki, David J. Lewis; John Morrison, project
manager; John Loercher, Kenneth Wong, Minna Choi, Elizabeth Kuwada,
Jason Dannenbring, Kevin Hayes, Keith Greenwald
Structural engineer: Robert Silman Associates

**ASCS E3 Science and Energy Park**, 2010–11, Norwalk, CT
Client: All Saints Catholic School, Amanda Gebicki, Alison Reilly
Project team: Paul Lewis, Marc Tsurumaki, David J. Lewis; Carrie Schulz
Contractor: CRS Carpentry, HousePro Construction Services

**New Taipei City Museum of Art Competition**, 2011, New Taipei City, Taiwan
Client: New Taipei City Government
Project team: Paul Lewis, Marc Tsurumaki, David J. Lewis; Raymond Bourraine,
Dave Freedman, Gabriel Jewell-Vitale, Tarlton Long, Kian Yam, Elizabeth Kuwada,
Kristen Chin, Erik Tsurumaki

**Claremont University Consortium Administrative Campus Center**

**Exhibit on Hollywood Boulevard**, *4 Projects: 4 Scales*, July 21–August 27, 2011, Los Angeles, CA
Client: Los Angeles Forum for Architecture and Urban Design
Project team: Paul Lewis, Marc Tsurumaki, David J. Lewis; John Morrison, Elizabeth Kuwada
Exhibit coordinator: Thurman Grant
LA Forum exhibit team: Jason Kerwin, Duane McLemore, Brian Daleidon, Khristeen Decastro, Anna Eremenko, Knarik Harutyunyan, Jason King, Jason Opp, Chris Parsell, Monica Ruiz, Oxana Yashenko, Kenneth Zapata
Sponsors: Woodbury University School of Architecture, Bartco Lighting, Corporate Contractors

**Meetup Offices**, 2010–11, New York, NY
Client: Meetup
Project team: Paul Lewis, Marc Tsurumaki, David J. Lewis; John Morrison, project manager; Hye-Young Chung, project manager; Kristen Chin, Elizabeth Kuwada, Eri Yamagata, David Temidara
Mechanical engineer: R.G. Vanderweil Engineers
Contractor: Qwest Contracting

**Claremont University Consortium Administrative Campus Center**, 2007–11, Claremont, CA
Client: Claremont University Consortium
Project team: Paul Lewis, Marc Tsurumaki, David J. Lewis; John Morrison, project manager; Hye-Young Chung, Perla Dís Kristindóttir, Michael Tyre, Matthew Clarke, Aaron Forrest, Deric Mizokami, Kevin Hayes, Tina Hunderup
Construction manager: CUC Construction Management and Facilities
Architect of record: Grant/Takacs Architecture
Structural engineer: John Labib and Associates
Mechanical engineer: CA Engineering Design Group

Civil engineer: Andreasen Engineering
Electrical engineer: Kocher Schirra Goharizi
Landscape architect: AHBE Landscape Architects
Lighting designer: LumenArch
LED artist: Jason Krugman
A/V consultant: TPI
LEED consultant: Ecotype Consulting

**Sullivan Family Student Center**, 2008–11, Laramie, WY
Client: College of Education, University of Wyoming
Project team: Paul Lewis, Marc Tsurumaki, David J. Lewis; Hye-Young Chung, project manager; Clark Manning, Matthew Clarke, Jason Dannenbring, Laura Cheung, John Morrison
Architect of record: University of Wyoming Facilities Planning Office
Structural engineer: Robert Silman Associates
Contractor: Elk Ridge Builders and Design
Topographic wall fabricator: Tietz-Baccon Design and Fabrication

**Opportunistic Architecture**, March 12–May 9, 2010, Mobile, AL
Client: Space 301
Project team: Paul Lewis, Marc Tsurumaki, David J. Lewis; Perla Dís Kristindóttir, Laura Cheung
Curator: Coleman Mills

**Arthouse at the Jones Center**, 2005–10, Austin, TX
Client: Arthouse at the Jones Center
Project team: Paul Lewis, Marc Tsurumaki, David J. Lewis; Jason Dannenbring, project manager; Michael Tyre, project manager; Matthew Roman, Laura Cheung, Monica Suberville, Hilary Zaic, Mia Lorenzetti, Tamicka Marcy, Eli Allen, Chris Cornecelli, Nicolas Rivard, Kristen Chin, Elena Koroleva, Aude Masboungi

## Sullivan Family Student Center

Structural engineer: MJ Structures
Mechanical engineer: Kent Consulting Engineers
Civil engineer: Garrett-Ihnen Civil Engineers
Lighting designer: LumenArch
LED lighting designer: Alejandro Bulaevsky
A/V consultant: Dickensheets Design Associates; Blue House Design, Media Integration
Contractor: Structura

**Spliced Townhouse**, 2005–7, 2008–10, New York, NY
Client: Constantine Alexakos
Project team: Paul Lewis, Marc Tsurumaki, David J. Lewis; Lucas Cascardo, project
    manager; Mia Lorenzetti, Matthew Roman (phase 1); John Morrison, project
    manager; Mia Lorenzetti Lee, Deric Mizokami, Kate Snider (phase 2)
Structural engineer: Robert Silman Associates
Mechanical engineer: D'Antonio Engineering
General contractor: Black Cat Construction (phase 1), J&J Johnson (phase 2)
Stair fabricator: Veyko (phase 1)

**Munchbar**, 2009–10, Bellevue, WA
Client: Private client
Project team: Paul Lewis, Marc Tsurumaki, David J. Lewis; Clark Manning, project
    manager; Jason Dannenbring, Laura Cheung, Mia Lorenzetti, Ed May, Kevin Hayes,
    Cody Fithian
Execuitve architect: Bergman Walls & Associates

**Royal Gardens Bakery**, 2009–10, Brooklyn, NY
Client: Private client
Project team: Paul Lewis, Marc Tsurumaki, David J. Lewis; Clark Manning,
    Perla Dís Kristinsdóttir, John Morrison, Cody Fithian

**Water Proving Ground**, *Rising Currents: Projects for New York's Waterfront*,
March 24–October 11, 2010, Museum of Modern Art, New York, NY
Client: Museum of Modern Art
Project team: Paul Lewis, Marc Tsurumaki, David J. Lewis; Aaron Forrest, Megan Griscom,
    Perla Dís Kristindóttir, Yasmin Vobis; Laura Cheung, John Morrison,
    Hye-Young Chung, Deric Mizokami, Cody Fithian, Mia Lorenzetti Lee,
    Jason Dannenbring, Clark Manning, Luke Smith, Yu-Cheng Koh, Amanda Kronk,
    Paul Landon, Phillip Chang, project assistants
Curator: Barry Bergdoll, Philip Johnson Chief Curator of Architecture and Design

**FreePlay Playground**, 2009
Client: FreePlay
Project team: Paul Lewis, Marc Tsurumaki, David J. Lewis; Matthew Clarke,
    Mia Lorenzetti, Annie Coombs

**The Buffet at MGM CityCenter**, 2006–9, Las Vegas, NV
Client: MGM Mirage CityCenter
Project team: Paul Lewis, Marc Tsurumaki, David J. Lewis; Clark Manning, project
    manager; Steven Hong, Tamicka Marcy, Hilary Zaic, Jason Dannenbring, Kristen
    Nakamura, Laura Cheung, Breanna Carlson
Architect of record: HKS
Mechanical engineer: Flack + Kurtz
Contractor: Perini Building Company

## Arthouse at the Jones Center

**Open Planning Project**, 2008–9, New York, NY
Client: Open Planning Project
Project team: Paul Lewis, Marc Tsurumaki, David J. Lewis; Clark Manning, Kate Snider, Perla Dís Kristindóttir, Eli Allen, Jason Dannenbring
Structural engineer: Gilsanz, Murray, Steficek
Mechanical engineer: Dagher Engineering
Lighting designer: LumenArch
Contractor: Qwest Contracting

**Department of Social and Cultural Analysis**, 2007–9, New York, NY
Client: New York University
Project team: Paul Lewis, Marc Tsurumaki, David J. Lewis; Clark Manning, project manager; Jason Dannenbring, Kristen Nakamura, Laura Cheung, Jason Andersen
Structural engineer: Robert Silman Associates
Mechanical engineer: Laszlo Bodak Engineer
Environmental graphics design: Design360
Lighting designer: Renfro Design Group
Contractor: R.P. Brennan

**The New School Social Space**, 2009, New York, NY
Client: The New School
Project team: Paul Lewis, Marc Tsurumaki, David J. Lewis; Perla Dís Kristindóttir
Contractor: Hunter Roberts

**Green Sponge/Greenwich South: A Vision for District-Wide Sustainability**, 2009, New York, NY
Client: Downtown Alliance
Commissioned by: Architecture Research Office
Project team: Paul Lewis, Marc Tsurumaki, David J. Lewis; Ryan Welch, Sunhwa Soh
Collaborator: David White

**Burns Townhouse**, 2005–8, Philadelphia, PA
Client: Jessica and Michael Burns
Project team: Paul Lewis, Marc Tsurumaki, David J. Lewis; Jason Dannenbring, project manager; Mia Lorenzetti Lee, Alex Terzich, Sheryl Bodine, Oscar Hernadez-Gomez
Structural engineer: Structural Design Associates
Contractor: Kevin Waggle

**Ordos Villa 93**, 2008, New York, NY
Client: Jiang Yuan Water Engineering
Project team: Paul Lewis, Marc Tsurumaki, David J. Lewis; Michael Tyre, Kate Snider, Deric Mizokami, Laura Cheung
Curator: Ai Weiwei/FAKE Design
Mechanical engineer: Arup

**Ludlow Hotel**, 2007–8, New York, NY
Client: S&H Equities
Project team: Paul Lewis, Marc Tsurumaki, David J. Lewis; Michael Tyre, project architect; John Morrison, project manager; Deric Mizokami, Laura Cheung, Susannah Brewster
Development consultant: Integrated Capital Consulting Group
Building architect: H. Thomas O'Hara Architects
Structural engineer: Robert Silman Associates
Mechanical engineer: Ettinger Engineering Associates
Contractor: Cava Construction

**Switchback House**, 2007–8, Akron, OH
Client: Private client
Project team: Paul Lewis, Marc Tsurumaki, David J. Lewis; Mia Lorenzetti, project manager; John Morrison, project manager; Hye-Young Chung, Clark Manning, Laura Cheung, Perla Dís Kristinsdóttir
Structural engineer: Robert Silman Associates

**Spliced Townhouse**

**Glenmore Gardens**, 2004–8, East New York, NY
Client: New York City Department of Housing Preservation and Development
Developer: Just Green, ET Partners with CPC Resources and
 Della Valle Bernheimer Development
Lead architect: Della Valle Bernheimer
Project team: Paul Lewis, Marc Tsurumaki, David J. Lewis; Eric Samuels, James Bennett,
 Lucas Cascardo
Collaborating firms: Architecture Research Office, BriggsKnowles Architecture + Design
Structural engineer: Robert Silman Associates
Contractor: Triple Crown Contracting

**Strategic Assessment, Planning and Design**, 2006–7, New York, NY
Client: New York University
Project team: Paul Lewis, Marc Tsurumaki, David J. Lewis; Mia Lorenzetti, project
 manager; Lucas Cascardo, project manager; Michael Tyre
Structural engineer: Robert Silman Associates
Mechanical engineer: Laszlo Bodak Engineer
Contractor: Plaza Construction

**Birdhouse**, 2007
Commissioned by: *I.D. Magazine*
Project team: Paul Lewis, Marc Tsurumaki, David J. Lewis; Diana Martinez

**The Grid and the Superblock**, 2007, New York, NY
Client: Friends of Hudson Square Design Charrette
Project team: Paul Lewis, Marc Tsurumaki, David J. Lewis; Clark Manning,
 Jason Dannenbring, Diana Martinez, Laura Cheung, Mia Lorenzetti
Curators: Michael Kramer, Stella Kramer

**Breath**, 2007, Avery Fisher Hall, Lincoln Center, New York, NY
Client: Lincoln Center
Project team: Paul Lewis, Marc Tsurumaki, David J. Lewis; Jason Dannenbring, project
 manager; Julian Rose, Clark Manning
Artist: Openended Group
Fabricator: Veyko

**New New York: Fast Forward**, March 29–May 7, 2007, Urban Center Galleries,
New York, NY
Client: Architectural League of New York
Project team: Paul Lewis, Marc Tsurumaki, David J. Lewis; Jason Dannenbring,
 Julian Rose, Clark Manning, Michael Tyre, Hilary Zaic, Tamicka Marcy,
 Mia Lorenzetti, Steven Hong, Kathryn Van Voorhees
Curators: Architectural League of New York; Gregory Wesner, Rosalie Genevro

**Kiku Sushi**, 2006–7, Navarre, FL
Client: Private client
Project team: Paul Lewis, Marc Tsurumaki, David J. Lewis; Michael Tyre, project manager;
 Mia Lorenzetti, project manager; Steven Hong, Matthew Clarke

**Garrido's Restaurant**, 2006–7, Austin, TX
Client: Michael Young and David Garrido
Project team: Paul Lewis, Marc Tsurumaki, David J. Lewis; Michael Tyre, Diana Martinez,
 Julian Rose, Lucas Cascardo, Mia Lorenzetti
Structural engineer: MJ Structures
Mechanical engineer: Kent Engineers

## The Buffet at MGM CityCenter

# Office Credits

Staff 2007–12

Jason Andersen
Sheryl Bodine
Phillip Chang
Constanza Cortes
Mercedes Cuvi
Oscar Hernandez-Gomez
Diana Mera Hernando
Amanda Kronk
Paul Landon
Sunhwa Soh
David Temidara
Yasmin Vobis
Ryan Welch
Kenneth Wong

**Emily Greene**
Gabriel Jewell-Vitale
Dave Freedman
Eri Yamagata
Steven Hong

**Matthew Storrie**
Raymond Bourraine
Kian Yam
Nicolas Rivard
Tina Hunderup

John Loercher
Tarlton Long
Mia Lorenzetti Lee

**Kristen Chin**
Deric Mizokami
Matthew Clarke

**Kevin Hayes**
Perla Dís Kristinsdóttir
Cody Fithian
Susannah Brewster
Diana Martinez

**Elizabeth Kuwada**
Angus McCullough
Chelsea Livingston
Laura Cheung

John Morriso
Michael Tyre

**Keith Greenw**
Hye-Young Ch

**Bold** = Current employee

Jason Dannenbring  Clark Manning

**Carrie Schulz**       **Kristen Alexander**
Aaron Forrest          Kristen Nakamura
Kate Snider            Elena Koroleva
Jeff White
Annie Coombs
Danielle Pecora
Kathryn Van Voorhees
Eli Allen

David J. Lewis       Marc Tsurumaki       Paul Lewis

# Professional Notes

## Books by LTL Architects:

2008 *Opportunistic Architecture*. New York: Princeton Architectural Press, 2008.

1998 *Pamphlet Architecture 21: Situation Normal...* New York: Princeton Architectural Press, 1998.

## Articles by LTL Architects:

2011 Tsurumaki, Marc. "Edge Incubator: Notes on Practice and Pedagogy." In *Testing to Failure: Design and Research in MIT's Department of Architecture*, edited by Sarah M. Hirschman, 396–99. Cambridge: SA+P, 2011.

2009 Tsurumaki, Marc. "Beyond?" In *Provisional: Emerging Modes of Architectural Practice USA*, edited by Elite Kedan, F. Jonathan Dreyfous, and Craig Mutter, 24–27. New York: Princeton Architectural Press, 2009.

2008 Lewis.Tsurumaki.Lewis. "Multivalent Performance in the Work of Lewis.Tsurumaki.Lewis." *Architectural Design* 78, no. 3 (May/June 2008): 46–53.

2007 Lewis.Tsurumaki.Lewis. "Mechanical Panoramas: Invernizzi's Il Girasole." *AA File*, no. 55 (Summer 2007): 30.

2006 Lewis.Tsurumaki.Lewis. "Decorative Dilemmas." In *Decoration*, edited by Emily Abruzzo and Jonathan D. Solomon, 20–21. New York: 306090, 2006.

2005 Lewis.Tsurumaki.Lewis. "Invernizzi's Exquisite Corpse: The Villa Girasole: An Architecture of Surrationalism." In *Surrealism and Architecture*, edited by Thomas Mical, 156–67. New York: Routledge, 2005.

Tsurumaki, Marc. "From the Known to the Unknown." *Volume* 1 (2005): 62–63.

2003 Lewis.Tsurumaki.Lewis. "Suburbanism of Mass Customization." *Cornell Journal of Architecture* 7 (2003): 34–43.

Lewis.Tsurumaki.Lewis. "Upside House: Speculative House Design for Etekt.com." *Center: A Journal for Architecture in America* (University of Texas), no. 12 (2003): 76–79.

2002 Lewis, David J. "Newness, Play, and Invention." *Scapes* 1 (2002): 20–21.

Lewis.Tsurumaki.Lewis. "Tourbus Hotel." In *Big Brother: Architecture and Surveillance*, 54–61. Athens: EMET, 2002.

2001 Lewis.Tsurumaki.Lewis. "New Suburbanism." *Ai: Architecture and Ideas* (Spring 2001): 72–79.

## Publications About LTL Architects:

2012 Born, Megan, et al, eds. *Dirt.* Philadelphia: PennDesign and The MIT Press, 2012. Water Proving Ground

Dickinson, Elizabeth. "Illuminated Ingenuity." *Architectural Lighting* (March/April 2012): 44–49. Arthouse

Farameh, Patrice, ed. *Go West! Cutting Edge Creatives in the United States.* Cologne, Germany: Daab Media GMBH, 2011.

Hawthorne, Christopher. "Screening Room." *Architectural Record* (February 2012): 80–83. Claremont University Consortium Administrative Campus Center

Lau, Wanda. "Lighten Up." *Eco-Structure* (January/February 2012): 21–23. Claremont University Consortium Administrative Campus Center

2011 Bergdoll, Barry. "Water Proving Ground." In *Rising Currents: Projects for New York's Waterfront*, edited by Barry Bergdoll, 80–89. New York: Museum of Modern Art, 2011.

Brake, Alan G. "A Learning Experience." *Interior Design* (March 2011): 220–27. Sullivan Family Student Center

de Monchaux, Thomas. "Keep Austin Adaptive." *Architect* (June 2011): 72–77. Arthouse

Hawthorne, Christopher. "Architecture Review: Administrative Campus Center at Claremont." *Los Angeles Times*, October 24, 2011.

Hightower, J. Brantley. "2011 Design Awards: Arthouse at the Jones Center." *Texas Architect* (September/October 2011): 44–47.

Johnson, Bernadette, ed. *Celebrating Excellence in Wood Structures: North American Wood Design Award Winners.* Ottawa: Canadian Wood Council, 2011. Arthouse

Martin, Earl, ed. *Knoll Textiles.* New Haven: Yale University Press, 2011. Parallel Lines Collection

McKeough, Tim. "Scaling Manhattan." *Azure* (March/April 2011): 35. Open Planning Project

Miller, Linda G. "Small Spaces, Transforming Results." *Oculus* (Fall 2011): 22. Sullivan Family Student Center

Spencer, Ingrid. "The Return to Reuse." *Architectural Record* (February 2011): 51–57. Arthouse

Woodward, Christopher. "The Age of Flower Towers." *Financial Times*, October 7, 2011. Green Sponge

2010 Brake, Alan G. "In the Swim." *The Architect's Newspaper*, April 7, 2010, 17–18. Water Proving Ground

Davidson, Justin. "When the Water Rises." *New York Magazine*, March 8, 2010, 28–31. Water Proving Ground

de Monchaux, Thomas. "Blue in Green: Notes on 'Rising Currents.'" *Log* 19 (2010): 79–86. Water Proving Ground

Faires, Robert. "Room for Possibility: Arthouse Creates a Space Where Artists Can Invent, Experiment, Make the Future." *Austin Chronicle*, October 22, 2010, 38.

Gronewald, Nathanial. "Architects Plan 'Amphibious Landscape' for New York City." *New York Times*, January 11, 2010. Water Proving Ground

Kristal, Marc. "Ini Ani Coffee Shop, New York, New York 2004." In *Re:Crafted: Interpretations of Craft in Contemporary Architecture and Interiors*, 62–67. New York: Monacelli, 2010.

Moreno, Shonquis, Robert Klanten, and Sven Ehmann, eds. "Lewis.Tsurumaki.Lewis—Tides and Fluff Bakery." In *Eat Out: Restaurant Design and Food Experiences*, 64–65, 226–27. Berlin: Die Gestalten Verlag, 2010.

"New York University Department of Social and Cultural Analysis." *MARU Interior Design* (May 2010): 64–72.

Rauen, Stacy Shoemaker. "CityCenter." *Hospitality Design* (April 2010): 177–88. The Buffet

"Rising Currents: Projects for New York's Waterfront to Respond to Climate Change." *Landscape Architecture China*, no. 3 (2010): 70–77. Water Proving Ground

van Ryzin, Jeanne Clair. "Arthouse Raises the Cultural Ante Downtown." *Austin American-Statesman*, October 17, 2010.

"Arthouse's Renovation Has Plenty of Curb Appeal." *Austin American-Statesman*, October 17, 2010.

2009 "LTL Architects: Lewis.Tsurumaki.Lewis: Experimentación, Representación y Material." *Polimorfo* 1 (2009): 88–97.

Kedan, Elite, F. Jonathan Dreyfous, and Craig Mutter, eds. *Provisional: Emerging Modes of Architectural Practice USA*. New York: Princeton Architectural Press, 2009.

Kellogg, Craig. "United, They Sit." *Interior Design* (September 2009): 214–21. Department of Social and Cultural Analysis

Wilk, Deborah. "The Rules Are...There Are No Rules." *Interior Design* (November 2009): 176–77. InterfaceFLOR/Interior Design Idea Lab 09 Installation

2008 Bell, Eugenia. "Design." *Frieze* (January/February 2008): 37–38. New New York

Blauvelt, Andrew. *Worlds Away: New Suburban Landscapes*. Minneapolis: Walker Art Center, 2008. New Suburbanism

Cadwell, Michael. "The Beauty of the Percolation: On the Interiors of Lewis Tsurumaki Lewis." *Harvard Design Magazine* (Fall / Winter 2008–9): 95–101.

"Fluff Bakery." *Color and Restaurant Design*. Barcelona: Loft Publications, 2008.

Galindo, Michelle. *1000X: Architecture of the Americas*, 140, 169. Berlin: Verlagshaus Braun, 2008. Arthouse and Glenmore Gardens

Hamin, Lee. "'NYU SAPD." *Bob* (December 2008): 150–51. Spliced Townhouse and Strategic Assessment, Planning and Design

Jodidio, Philip. *100 Contemporary Architects*. Köln: Taschen, 2008. 537–40. Fluff Bakery

Kolarevic, Branko and Kevin R. Klinger. *Manufacturing Material Effects: Rethinking Design and Making in Architecture*. London: Routledge, 2008.

Man, Chan Wing. "More Than Design." *Eat & Travel Weekly* (November 2008): 118–21.

Sokol, David. "Teaching by Example: Design-Build Educators Talk Pedagogy and Realpolitik." *Architectural Record* (October 2008): 120–26.

Tasarim, Mimari. "Fluff Bakery." *Yapi* (March 2008): 100–3.

2007 Broto, Carles. *Restaurants, Cafes & Bars*. Barcelona: Links, 2007. Fluff Bakery and Xing Restaurant

Cullerton, Erin and Michelle Galindo, eds. *Young Architects Americas*. New York: Daab, 2007. Bornhuetter Hall and Xing Restaurant

Einik, Nurit. *Knoll Textiles: 60 Years of Modern Design*. Berlin: Knoll, 2007. Parallel Lines Collection

Engelhorn, Beate. *Young Americans: New Architecture in the USA*. Berlin: DOM, 2007. Bornhuetter Hall, Tides Restaurant, and Fluff Bakery

"Foro de Arquitectura, New (York) Architects." *ION+* (2007): 92–97.

Hudson, Jennifer. *Interior Architecture Now*, 154–59. London: Laurence King, 2007.

"Interieur Sauce Design." *AMC* (February 2007): 88–91. Fluff Bakery

Khemsurov, Monica. "Messing with Perfection: Eight Proposals to Ornament the Farnsworth House." *I.D.* (March / April 2007): 76–83. Bird House

McDonald, Shannon S. *The Parking Garage: Design and Evolution of a Modern Urban Form*. Washington, DC: Urban Land Institute, 2007. Park Tower

Milovanovic-Bertram, Smilja. *Lessons from Rome: The Work of Robert Venturi, Tod Williams, Thomas Phifer, and Paul Lewis*, 83–113. Austin: University of Texas at Austin, 2007.

Nobel, Philip. "Awards: In Design Awards, Something Old And Something New." *New York Times*, May 17, 2007.

"Ofenfrisch." *AIT* (September 2007): 92–97. Fluff Bakery

Seward, Aaron. "Design Comes Home." *The Architect's Newspaper*, April 25, 2007, 30–32.

Volner, Ian. "Lewis.Tsurumaki.Lewis: Opportunistic Architecture." *Architectural Record* (December 2007): 55–56.

Weiss, Sean. "Xing Restaurant." In *New York: Architecture & Design*, 138–39. New York: teNeues, 2007.

Yelavich, Susan. *Contemporary World Interiors*. New York: Phaidon, 2007. Lozoo Restaurant, Fluff Bakery, and Tides Restaurant

Zeiger, Mimi. "More for Less." *Azure* (September 2007): 116–25. Glenmore Gardens

2006 Busquets, Joan, and Felipe Correa, eds. *Cities: 10 Lines—A New Lens for the Urbanistic Project*, 316–19. Cambridge: Harvard University Graduate School of Design, 2006. Park Tower and New Suburbanism

Chen, Aric. "Experimental Architects Draft New Looks for the Wall." *New York Times*, June 29, 2006. Parallel Lines Collection

"Effect > fast food > dash dogs // new york." *Monitor*, no. 37 (2006): 94–97.

"Follow the Ribbon." *Mark*, no. 4 (Fall 2006): 53. Xing Restaurant

Gardiner, Virginia. "Design, Build, and Beyond." *Dwell* (February / March 2006): 152–64.

Jodidio, Philip. "Xing Restaurant" and "Arthouse at the Jones Center." In *Architecture in the United States*, 98–107. London: Taschen, 2006.

Jodidio, Philip. "Dash Dogs." In *Minimum Space Maximum Living*, 50–53. Victoria: Images Publishing Group, 2006.

Jodidio, Philip. "Fluff Bakery" and "Bornhuetter Hall." In *Architecture Now 4*, 274–381. London: Taschen, 2006.

Kasuga, Yoshiko. "Dash Dogs." *SPA-DE: Space and Design* 5 (2006): 116–17.

Lim, CJ. "Bellow.Lewis.Tsurumaki.Lewis" and "Eavesdropping.Lewis. Tsurumaki.Lewis." In *Devices: A Manual of Architectural and Spatial Machines*, 28–29, 64–65. Oxford: Architectural Press, 2006.

Marull, Kina. "Panaderia Fluff." *Diseñ Art Magazine*, no. 7 (2006): 158–59.

Moreno, Shonquis. "Dash In, Dash Out." *Frame*, no. 50 (May / June 2006): 40. Dash Dogs

Riordan, John. "Tides" and "Xing." In *Restaurants by Design*, 16–23, 92–99. New York: Collins Design, 2006.

"Scope: Fluff Bakery, Tides Restaurant, Xing Restaurant." *IW Magazine* (Taiwan), (Summer 2006): 52–64.

Von Arx, Irina. "Il cuoco, l'artigiano e l'architetto." *Domus* (April 2006): 42–47. Dash Dogs and Xing Restaurant

Weathersby, Jr., William. "Lewis.Tsurumaki.Lewis Turns the Tables on an Oddly Shaped Space Fashioning Xing in New York City." *Architectural Record* (March 2006): 187, 198–201. Xing Restaurant

"The Writing's on the Wallpaper." *Architectural Record* (August 2006): 191. Parallel Lines Collection

2005 "03: Food > Fluff Bakery // New York." *Monitor*, no. 30 (2005): 34–37.

"Architectural Design: restaurant > Tides // New York." *Monitor*, no. 32 (2005): 62–65.

"Art to Go." *Better Homes and Gardens* (September 2005): 144. Ini Ani Coffee Shop

Braham, Bill. "Zoom In: Ivalo Lighting: Ivalo > Rotare." *Monitor*, no. 33 (2005): 100–01.

"Generic Chic." *Newsweek*, August 1, 2005, 57–58. Prototype Dormitory Room

Gregory, Rob. "Shifting Tides." *Architectural Review* (December 2005): 85. Tides Restaurant

Gross, Jamie. "Winning Streaks." *Surface*, no. 53 (2005): 60. Fluff Bakery

Hagberg, Eva. "Currents: To Protect Their Projects, Young Architects Try DIY." *New York Times*, March 10, 2005. Tides Restaurant and Xing Restaurant

Hall, Peter. "Rotare: Lewis.Tsurumaki.Lewis." *Metropolis* (June 2005): 180–81.

Kagelmann, Boris. "From Inside to Out." *Jam* (Autumn / Winter 2005): 4–9.

Kasuga, Yoshiko. "Fluff Bakery." *SPA-DE: Space and Design* 3 (2005): 45–47.

"Tides," and "Xing." *SPA-DE: Space and Design* 4 (2005): 75–81.

Kunz, Martin Nicholas. *Cafe & Restaurant Design*. New York: teNeues, 2005. Ini Ani Coffee Shop

"Lewis.Tsurumaki.Lewis: Architectural Opportunism." *Dimensions* (University of Michigan) 18 (2005): 88–95.

"Lewis.Tsurumaki.Lewis: Xing Restaurant, Fluff Bakery, Ini Ani Coffee Shop, Bornhuetter Hall." *MARU Interior Design* (April 2004): 50–65.

Mastrelli, Tara. "Horizontal Vertigo." *Hospitality Design* (April 2005): 164–67. Fluff Bakery

McKee, Bradford. "The New College Mixer." *New York Times*, September 1, 2005. Bornhuetter Hall

McKeough, Tim. "In Three Manhattan Restaurants." *Icon*, no. 25 (July 2005): 39–40. Fluff Bakery, Tides Restaurant, and Xing Restaurant

Moreno, Shonquis. "The Space: The Literal Zone." *Frame*, no. 46 (September / October 2005): 154–57. Tides Restaurant

Pogrebin, Robin. "New York's New Architecture District." *New York Times*, August 21, 2005. Essex Street Studios

Ryan, Zoë. "Detail 01: Bread and Butter." *Frame* 44 (May/June 2005): 21–22. Fluff Bakery

Seward, Aaron. "Dining Duo, New York City." *Architectural Lighting* (May/June 2005): 48–49. Fluff Bakery and Xing Restaurant

Singh, Karen D. "Labworks, Materials Study: Lewis.Tsurumaki.Lewis." *Interior Design* (March 2005): 121–22. Xing Restaurant

"Wave of the Future." *Hospitality Design* (October 2005): 114–27.

Wines, Suzan. "Dionysius in New York." *Domus Speciale* (April 2005): 34–39.

Yang, Andrew. "Triple Ingenuity." *Metropolis* (May 2005): 140–44. Fluff Bakery, Tides Restaurant, and Xing Restaurant

2004 "Bar en Carton." *Le Moniteur Architecture* (October 2004): 38. Ini Ani Coffee Shop

Blair, Gwenda. "Designers Redefine the Political Machine." *New York Times*, October 7, 2004. Bellow

Cuito, Aurora. "Lozoo Restaurant" and "Geltner/Parker Loft." In *New York Minimalism*, 48–53, 118–25. New York: Harper Design International, 2004.

Fischer, Joachim, ed. "Lozoo Restaurant." In *Restaurant Design*, 254–63. Köln: Daab, 2004.

Galadza, Sofia. "Material: In the Mix." *Contract* (December 2004): 30–31. Tides Restaurant and Xing Restaurant

"Geltner/Parker Loft." In *New Kitchen Design*, 112–15. Köln: Daab, 2004.

Holtzman, Anna. "Interior Design, No Appointment Necessary." *New York Times*, April 15, 2004. Ini Ani Coffee Shop

"Hydrogen Park Tower." *H2CarsBiz2*, no. 4 (2004): 16–17. Park Tower

Ivy, Robert. "On the Road to Venice: 9th Architecture Biennale." *Architectural Record* (November 2004): 91–119. Parking Sections

Kasuga, Yoshiko. "Ini Ani Coffee Shop." *SPA-DE: Space and Design* 2 (2004): 106–8.

Kristal, Marc. "Divide and Conquer." *Metropolis* (May 2004): 74–78. Essex Street Studios

"Lozoo Restaurant." *Lighting Today* 1 (2004): 50–53.

Minutillo, Josephine. "Share and Share I Like: Essex Street Studio." *Architectural Record* (January 2004): 50.

Pearson, Clifford A. "For the Pint-Size Ini Ani Coffee Shop in Lower Manhattan, Lewis.Tsurumaki.Lewis Reinvents the Java-Sipping Experience." *Architectural Record* (September 2004): 118–21.

Serrats, Marta. "Geltner/Parker Loft." In *Big Designs for Small Kitchens*, 36–39. New York: Harper Design International, 2004.

Yang, Andrew. "The New New Yorkers." *Surface*, no. 50 (October 2004): 150.

2003 Adam, Huburtus. "Van Alen Institute" and "Lozoo." In *New York Architecture and Design*, 52–53, 120–21. New York: teNeues, 2003.

Brown, Bay. "Lewis.Tsurumaki.Lewis: Grand Egyptian Museum Competition." *Architecture* (May 2003): 62–63.

Kristal, Marc. "Linear Solution." *Metropolis* (October 2003): 44. Lozoo Restaurant

"Lozoo Chinese Kitchen." *I.D. Magazine 49 Annual Design Review* (July/August 2003): 119.

Luna, Ian. "Lozoo" and "Van Alen Institute." In *New New York: Architecture and a City*, 74–77, 120–23. New York: Rizzoli, 2003.

Smiley, David J. "A Vertical Mixed-Use Suburb." In *Sprawl and Public Space, Readdressing the Mall*, 74–75. Washington, DC: NEA, 2003. New Suburbanism

Yang, Andrew. "04-Off the Shoulder." *Frame* (March/April 2003): 24. Lozoo Restaurant

2002 Albrecht, Donald, and Elizabeth Johnson. "Lewis.Tsurumaki.Lewis. Tourbus Hotel." In *New Hotels for Global Nomads*, 76–79. New York: Merrel, 2002.

Filippis, Memos. "Big Brother, Architecture and Surveillance: Effective Affinities." In *Big Brother: Architecture and Surveillance*, 11–24. Athens: EMET, 2002. Tourbus Hotel

Hays, K. Michael, and Lauren Kogod, eds. "Twenty Projects at the Boundaries of the Architectural Discipline Examined in Relation to the Historical and Contemporary Debates Over Autonomy." *Perspecta* 33 (2002): 54–71. New Suburbanism

Turner, Rob. "Keeping the Lighting Turned Up and the Budget Down." *New York Times*, October 17, 2002. Lozoo Restaurant

2001 Bell, Jonathan. "Destination Unknown." In *Carchitecture*, 122–23. Basel: Birkhauser, 2001. New Suburbanism and Tourbus Hotel

"Interview with Lewis.Tsurumaki.Lewis." *Van Alen Report* 9 (May 2001): 9–25.

Muschamp, Herbert. "Instant Inspiration: Just Add Water." *New York Times*, April 6, 2001. Architecture + Water

"No Reservations." *Interiors* (March 2001): 100–1. Prototype Hotel Room

Rappaport, Nina. "An Architecture in the Making: Young Architects in New York." *TEC21* 8 (February 23, 2001): 7–18. Slip Space, Lozoo Restaurant, and Refiled

Sirefman, Susanna. *New York: A Guide to Recent Architecture*. London: Ellipsis, 2001: 5.4–5.5. Van Alen Institute

2000 Albrecht, Donald, Ellen Lupton, and Steven Skov Holt. *Design Culture Now: National Design Triennial*. New York: Princeton Architectural Press, 2000: 134–35.

Stephens, Suzanne. "Design Vanguard: Lewis.Tsurumaki.Lewis Explores Ways of Making the Familiar Strange." *Architectural Record* (December 2000): 116–99.

1999 "Division of Labour." *Architectural Review* (July 1999): 86–87. Van Alen Institute

Kellogg, Craig. "Offices that Work: Modular Squad." *Working Woman* (February 1999): 58. Princeton Architectural Press Offices

Schwartz, Bonnie. "The Van Alen Effect." *Interiors* (October 1999): 64–65. Van Alen Institute

"Van Alen Institute." *I.D. Magazine 45 Annual Design Review* (July/August 1999): 179.

1997 Codrington, Andrea. "'Pull of Beauty' at the Storefront for Art and Architecture." *I.D. Magazine 43 Annual Design Review* (July/August 1997): 149.

"'Eavesdropping' at Exit Art: The First World." *I.D. Magazine 43 Annual Design Review* (July/August 1997): 154.

1995 "Slipping Space at Storefront." *I.D. Magazine 41 Annual Design Review* (July/August 1995): 148–50.

**Select Firm Awards:**

2010  Lawrence Israel Prize, Fashion Institute of Technology

2007  National Design Award, Interior Design, Cooper-Hewitt, National
Design Museum

2004  Selected Architects, Venice Biennale—U.S. Pavilion

2002  Selected Architects, Emerging Voices, Architectural League of New York

2000  Selected Architects, "The New Vanguard," *Architectural Record*
Award and Grant, New York Foundation for the Arts

1997  Selected Architect, Young Architects Forum, Architectural League of
New York

**Select Project Awards:**

2012  AIA Design Merit Award, Urban Design, New York Chapter.
Water Proving Ground

Lumen Award of Merit, Illuminating Engineering Society NYC.
Claremont University Consortium

Excellence in Design Award, Renovation, Claremont Architectural
Commission. Claremont University Consortium

2011  AZ Award Finalist, Unrealized Concept, *Azure.* Water Proving Ground

Best of Year Merit Award, Educational, *Interior Design.*
Sullivan Family Student Center

AIA Design Award, Project, Texas Society of Architects. Arthouse

Lumen Award of Excellence, Illuminating Engineering Society NYC.
Arthouse

2010  Citation Winner, Wood Design & Building. Arthouse

Outstanding Construction Award, Specialty Construction, with Structura,
Austin Chapter AGC. Arthouse

2008  Best of Year Merit Award, Educational, *Interior Design.* Department of
Social and Cultural Analysis

2007  Building Brooklyn Award, Affordable Housing, Brooklyn Chamber of
Commerce. Glenmore Gardens

2006  Outstanding Restaurant Design, James Beard Foundation Award.
Xing Restaurant

AIA Design Award, Project Citation, New York Chapter. Nazareth House

2005  Winner, Casual Restaurant, First Annual Hospitality Design Awards for
Creative Achievement, *Hospitality Design.* Fluff Bakery

Honorable Mention, Casual Restaurant, Second Annual Hospitality Design
Awards for Creative Achievements, *Hospitality Design.* Dash Dogs

Finalist, Casual Dining, Gold Key Awards, *Interior Design.* Tides Restaurant
and Fluff Bakery

2004  Design Distinction, Environments, *I.D. Magazine* 51st Annual Design Review.
Ini Ani Coffee Shop

Winner, Interiors Awards, Restaurant, *Contract.* Tides Restaurant

AIA Design Merit Award, Interior Architecture, AIA New York Chapter.
Xing Restaurant

AIA Design Merit Award, Projects, New York Chapter. Park Tower

Honorable Mention, AR Awards for Emerging Architecture, *Architectural
Review.* Tides Restaurant

Interiors Award Winner, Restaurant, *Contract.* Ini Ani Coffee Shop

2003  James Beard Foundation Award Nomination, Outstanding Restaurant Design.
Lozoo Restaurant

2002  Design Distinction, Environments, *I.D. Magazine* 49th Annual Design Review.
Lozoo Restaurant

Kalil Memorial Fellowship, to support research on Invernizzi's
Girasole, Verona

New Suburbanism installed in the permanent collection, Heinz
Architectural Center at the Carnegie Museum of Art

2000  Faculty Design Award, Associate of Collegiate Schools of Architecture,
Van Alen Institute

New Suburbanism installed in the permanent collection, Architecture and
Design, San Francisco Museum of Modern Art

1999  Sportbars and Mies-on-a-Beam installed in the permanent collection,
Architecture and Design, San Francisco Museum of Modern Art

Design Distinction, Environments, *I.D. Magazine* 45th Annual Design Review.
Van Alen Institute

Mercedes T. Bass Rome Prize in Architecture, American Academy in Rome,
1998–99. Paul Lewis

1997  Design Distinction, Environments, *I.D. Magazine* 43rd Annual Design Review.
Pull of Beauty

Design Distinction, Environments, *I.D. Magazine* 43rd Annual Design Review.
Eavesdropping

1995  Best of Category, Environments, *I.D. Magazine* 41st Annual Design Review.
Slip Space

## Exhibitions:

2012  *LTL Architects–Exhibition.* College of Wooster Art Museum, Wooster, OH
*LTL Architects–Recent Work.* Roger Williams University, Bristol, RI
*LTL Architects–Recent Work.* University of California, Berkeley
*The Way Beyond Art 3: Architecture in the Expanded Field.* CCA Wattis Institute for Contemporary Arts, San Francisco, CA

2011  *4 Projects: 4 Scales–LTL Architects.* Los Angeles Forum for Architecture and Urban Design
*Knoll Textiles: 1945–2010.* Bard Graduate Center, New York, NY

2010  *Rising Currents: Projects for New York's Waterfront.* Museum of Modern Art, New York, NY
*75 Years of Looking Forward.* San Francisco Museum of Modern Art
*Design USA: Contemporary Innovation.* Cooper-Hewitt, National Design Museum, New York, NY
*Opportunistic Architecture.* Space 301, Mobile, AL

2009  *America / Ordos.* Bridge 8 Cultural Center, Shanghai, China
*InterfaceFLOR / Interior Design Idea Lab 09.* InterfaceFLOR Aware House, LaGrange, GA
*What If?* Center for Architecture, New York, NY
*Recent Work of LTL Architects.* Syracuse University, Syracuse, NY
*Five Principles for Greenwich South.* Alliance for Downtown New York, Zuccotti Park, New York, NY

2008  *13:100: Thirteen New York Architects Design for Ordos.* Architectural League of New York, Urban Center Galleries, New York, NY
*Worlds Away: New Suburban Landscapes.* Walker Art Center, Minneapolis, MN
*Cut: Revealing the Section.* San Francisco Museum of Modern Art
*Lessons from Rome.* University of Texas at Austin

2007  *Breath.* Avery Fisher Hall, Lincoln Center, New York, NY
*New New York.* Architectural League of New York, Urban Center Galleries, New York, NY

2006  *Light Structures.* Kent State University, Kent, OH
*Very Recent Work.* Icebox Gallery, Syracuse, NY
*The Green House.* National Building Museum, New York, NY
*Transcending Type.* Yale School of Architecture Gallery, New Haven, CT

2005  *Restricted Play.* Parsons The New School for Design, New York, NY
*Light Structures.* Northeastern University, Boston, MA
*Cities: 10 Lines. Approaches to City and Open Territory Design.* Harvard University Graduate School of Design, Cambridge, MA

2004  *Light Structures.* University of Michigan, Ann Arbor, MI
*Parking Sections,* U.S. Pavilion, Venice Biennale. 9th International Architecture Exhibition, Venice, Italy
*Voting Booth Project.* Parsons The New School for Design, New York, NY

2003  *FAAR-Out: Six Months in Rome.* Art Directors Club, New York, NY
*Light Structures.* Syracuse University, Syracuse, NY

2002  *Architecture + Water.* University of California, Los Angeles, San Francisco Museum of Modern Art, Heinz Architectural Center, Carnegie Museum of Art, Pittsburgh, PA
*Negotiating Domesticity: Inquiry into Contemporary Suburban Residential Design.* Greenwich Arts Council, Greenwich, CT
*Big Brother: Architecture and Surveillance.* National Museum of Contemporary Art, Athens, Greece
*Three Dimensions of Architecture.* The Rachofsky House, Dallas, TX
*Satirical Efficiencies.* University of Virginia, Charlottesville, VA
*2x2.* University of Texas at Austin
*New Hotels for Global Nomads.* Cooper-Hewitt, National Design Museum, New York, NY

2001  *Snafu.* University of Pennsylvania School of Architecture, Dean's Gallery, Philadelphia, PA
*Architecture + Water.* Van Alen Institute, New York, NY

2000  *Experiments: Recent Acquisitions of the Permanent Collection of Architecture and Design.* San Francisco Museum of Modern Art
*Faculty Exhibit.* Cornell University, Hartell Gallery, Cornell, NY
*Refiled, National Design Triennial.* Cooper-Hewitt, National Design Museum, New York, NY
*10 Shades of Green.* Architectural League of New York, Urban Center Galleries, New York, NY

1999  *Snafu.* Parsons The New School for Design, New York, NY
*ReInstalled.* AAM Architettura Arte Moderna, Rome, Italy
*Three Rome Speculations.* American Academy in Rome, Italy

1998  *Architecture @ the Edge of the Millennium,* American Academy in Rome, Italy and New York, NY

1997  *Mantel Piece.* Urban Center Galleries, New York, NY
*Testing 1…2…3…* Storefront for Art and Architecture, New York, NY

1996  *Eavesdropping.* Exit Art: The First World, New York, NY
*Pull of Beauty.* Storefront for Art and Architecture, New York, NY

1994  *Slip Space.* Storefront for Art and Architecture, New York, NY

**Lectures:**

2012 AIA National Convention, Washington, DC
Boston Architectural College
College of Wooster
Louisiana State University
Roger Williams University
University of California, Berkeley
University of Hong Kong
University of Michigan

2011 AIA Louisiana, Baton Rouge
AIA Wisconsin Convention, Madison
Association of Icelandic Architects
Marywood University
Rice University
Temple University
Texas A&M University
University of California, Los Angeles
University of Pennsylvania
Wright Lecture Series, Madison

2010 AIA Central Pennsylvania, Harrisburg
AIA Colorado Convention, Denver
AIA National Convention, Miami
Blouin Creative Leadership Summit
Cooper Union
Cornell University
Fashion Institute of Technology
Massachusetts Institute of Technology
Museum of Modern Art
Ohio State University
Oklahoma State University
Parsons The New School for Design
Southern Polytechnic State University
Texas Tech University
University of Texas at Arlington
University of Wisconsin, Milwaukee
Woodbury University
Wright at 100 Steelcase

2009 AIA Minnesota Convention, Minneapolis
AIA National Convention, San Francisco
Black Rock Design Institute
California College of the Arts
Culintro Culinary Trade Organization
Drury University
Forum for Urban Design
Los Angeles Museum of Contemporary Art
Otis College of Art and Design
Syracuse University
University of Arizona
University of Michigan
United States Green Building Council

2008 Arthouse at the Jones Center
Carnegie Mellon University
Florida International University
Polytechnic University of Puerto Rico
Tulane Univeristy
University of Arkansas
University of Limerick
University of North Carolina at Charlotte

2007 Ball State University
Carleton University
Harvard University
Cooper-Hewitt, National Design Museum
New Jersey Institute of Technology
AIA New York
Parsons The New School for Design
Sci-Fi Design, Milan, Italy
Universidad San Francisco de Quito, Ecuador
University of Kansas
University of Maryland
Washington University in St. Louis
Yale University

2006 AIA Florida Emerging Professionals Conference
Autonomous University of Nuevo Leon, Mexico
California Polytechnic State University
Catholic University of America
Kent State University
Louisiana Tech University
North Carolina State University
Rice University
University of British Columbia
University of Nebraska
University of Oklahoma
Virginia Commonwealth University
Yale University

2005 ACSA Keynote Lecture, Detroit
Architecture Talks, Lucerne, Switzerland
AIA Baltimore
Dallas Architecture Forum
DDI Color Material Specifiers Conference
Florida Atlantic University
Georgia Institute of Technology
Lawrence Technological University
Miami University, Ohio
New York Designs, Architectural League of New York
Northeastern University
Parsons The New School for Design
University at Buffalo, State University of New York
University of Colorado
University of Tennessee
University of Texas at Austin
Wesleyan University

2004 Colorado College
Columbia University
Princeton University
University of Michigan

2003 Architectural Association of Ireland
California College of the Arts
Denver Architectural Lab
Kansas City AIA Young Architects Forum
Pennsylvania State University
Pratt Institute
San Francisco Museum of Modern Art
Syracuse University
University of North Carolina at Chapel Hill
Virginia Polytechnic Institute
Young Architect Forum, Copenhagen, Denmark

2002 Emerging Voices, Architectural League of New York
Carnegie Museum of Art
Cooper Union
Rhode Island School of Design
Southern California Institute of Architecture
University of California, Berkeley
University of Nevada, Las Vegas
University of Texas at Austin
University of Toronto
University of Virginia

2001 Nashville Cultural Arts Project
Ohio State University
Stony Brook, State University of New York
University of Oregon, Portland
University of Oregon, Eugene
University of Pennsylvania
Van Alen Institute

2000 Catholic University of America
Drury University
New Jersey Institute of Technology
New York University

1999 American Academy in Rome
Temple University

# Acknowledgments

The work in this publication is very much a product of the diligence, talents, and capabilities of the extraordinary group of individuals who have been an integral part of the collaborative office of LTL Architects. Over the years, they have shown their abilities to greet the challenges of practicing architecture with an appropriate admixture of intensity and humor, endurance and enthusiasm. We are especially grateful for the long-standing dedication of the associates in the office—Clark Manning, John Morrison, Jason Dannenbring, and Michael Tyre—who consistently take the lead in ensuring that projects are executed with a combination of invention and precision.

As professionals and educators, we offer our appreciation to our students for their dialogue and investigations into the potentials of architecture. Through our academic roles at Princeton University, Columbia University, and Parsons The New School for Design, as well as visiting studios at a variety of architectural programs, we have benefited greatly from the exchanges and friendships with our colleagues, including Kimberly Ackert, Lucia Allais, Stan Allen, Amale Andraos, Sunil Bald, Michael Bell, Andy Bernheimer, Stella Betts, Christine Boyer, Laura Briggs, Hillary Brown, Merritt Bucholz, Eric Bunge, Michael Cadwell, Peter Carroll, Gerard Carty, Stephen Cassell, Terri Chiao, Beatriz Colomina, Yolande Daniels, Jared Della Valle, Elizabeth Diller, Edward Eigen, Karen Fairbanks, Natalie Fizer, Morgan Flynn, Jan Frohburg, Mario Gandelsonas, Jean Gardner, Leslie Gill, Paul Golberger, Gráinne Hassett, Elizabeth Hatz, Mimi Hoang, Eric Höweler, Axel Kilian, Kent Kleinman, Jonathan Knowles, Alexis Kraft, Marc Kushner, David Leven, Giuseppe Lignano, Astrid Lipka, Michael Manfredi, Scott Marble, Reinhold Martin, Jonathan Marvel, Ed May, Tim McDonald, Karen McEvoy, John McMorrough, Michael Meredith, Joanna Merwood-Salisbury, Ana Miljački, John Miller, John Mitchell, Guy Nordenson, Nat Oppenheimer, Spyridon Papapetros, Peter Pelsinski, David Piscuskas, Derek Porter, Mark Rakatansky, Mahadev Raman, Jesse Reiser, Lyn Rice, Juergen Riehm, Mark Robbins, Rob Rogers, Richard Rosa, Lindy Roy, Jonsara Ruth, Hilary Sample, Joel Sanders, Catherine Seavitt, Andrea Simitch, Hayes Slade, James Slade, Joel Stoehr, Karen Stonely, Nader Tehrani, Ada Tolla, Joel Towers, Kazys Varnelis, Anthony Vidler, Enrique Walker, Val Warke, Marion Weiss, Sandra Wheeler, Peter Wheelwright, David White, Sarah Whiting, Mark Wigley, Ron Witte, Dan Wood, Adam Yarinsky, J. Meejin Yoon, and Alfred Zollinger.

We are indebted to our clients and sponsors for their continued support, insight, and critical engagement, without which we would not be able to realize these projects. In this regard, we offer particular gratitude to Constantine Alexakos, Cindy Allen, Sven Van Assche, Hansel Bauman, Barry Bergdoll, Mary Brabeck, Jessica and Michael Burns, Rosalie Genevro, Sue Graze, Stephen Jones, Jeanne and Michael Klein, Lori Mazor, Sarah Patton, Nancy Rosen, and Robert Walton.

Special thanks to Kevin Lippert of Princeton Architectural Press for his many years of support, to editorial assistant Gina Morrow for her careful attention to details, and to editor Megan Carey for her critical eye and skillful shepherding of the book to fruition. We are grateful for seventeen years of collaboration with the photographer Michael Moran, whose exceptional work fills these pages. This book would not have been possible without Elizabeth Kuwada's precise, iterative work with the graphic design.

And finally, we remain grateful for the continued support of our families—Daina Tsurumaki, Toshi Tsurumaki, Chris Tsurumaki, Beth Irwin Lewis, Arnold Lewis, and Martha Lewis.

This book is dedicated to:
Kim Yao, Sarabeth Lewis Yao,
and Maximo Lewis Yao
—Paul Lewis
Carmen Lenzi, Kai Luca Tsurumaki,
and Lucia Alise Tsurumaki
—Marc Tsurumaki
Alice Min Soo Chun
and Quinn Arnold Lewis
—David J. Lewis